AF559622

ADVANCED JOURNALISM

ADVANCED JOURNALISM

Including MID-DAY Sunshine

(Revised Edition)

Adarsh Kumar Varma

HAR–ANAND PUBLICATIONS PVT LTD
E-49/3, Okhla Industrial Area, Phase-II, New Delhi-110020
Tel.: 41603490 Fax: 011-41708607
E-mail: info@haranandpublications.com
Website: www.haranandpublications.com

Revised Edition, 2001

Reprint, 2015

Published by Ashok Gosain and Ashish Gosain for
Har-Anand Publications Pvt Ltd

Printed in India at Vishal Binding House

Acknowledgments

The Debts I Owe

This study is largely based on personal experience supplemented by meetings with many of the distinguished media persons whose achievements it tries to learn from.

In some cases, the transcripts were passed on to the distinguished persons concerned to check and correct errors of fact, date, etc. Among those who extended such cooperation are Mr. Kuldip Nayar, Mr. S. Nihal Singh, Mr. K.P.K. Kutty, Mr. Virendra Mohan and Mr. R.D. Kwatra.

Mr. Nayar—all credit to him—spared the time to go through the two chapters referred to him and to correct some of the facts though he had to go out on a professional assignment. Mr. Nihal Singh, as everyone has come to expect from him, burnt the midnight oil to look at the portion referred to him and returned it the next morning.

Mr. Kutty and Mr. Virendra Mohan dug up lots of facts—from memory and from UNI's archives—to give me invaluable data of which I was only vaguely aware. Apart from this, there was one whole day when they allowed me to park myself in their office in UNI, plying me with endless cups of coffee, and telling me verbally of many things even as they went about running a busy news agency. There were many occasions when our conversation was interrupted in mid-sentence as major news requiring their attention broke. One of them was the hijacking of an Indian Airlines flight! Yet, not for a moment did they allow me to feel unwanted. All glory to them.

Mr. Kwatra, who is part of the pantheon of professional gurus I have collected over three decades and more, and who handpicked me to succeed him at the *Pioneer* in 1984 from hundreds of journalists he has worked with, volunteered to go through not only *The Pioneer Story* but through the entire manuscript. This at age 80, and most willingly. He clarified many of the issues that were involved in the *Pioneer* succession and which I had imperfectly understood. He also took pains to suggest corrections in spellings, names, facts, dates, etc, in other parts of the transcript.

As a matter of clarification, my pantheon of gurus includes the late Mr. M. Chalapathi Rau and others whose list is too long to write here. However, one name I cannot resist mentioning. It is Mr. Kanhaiya Lal, the very first foreman I worked with. He told an impetuous and ignorant young man what make-up is!

Mr. Sudhir Dar, whom I have known since our college days and with whom I worked in the *Statesman* for three years, bore with me for more than an hour giving facts, dates, quotes, etc, regarding his *Out of My Mind* and correcting a few wrong impressions that I had.

I acknowledge with gratitude the fraternal help given by these people and by several others. It is a measure of their professional discipline and consideration for a colleague that none of them ever tried to meddle or argue with the opinions expressed in the manuscript, which remain my very own. Similarly, if any errors of fact or date still remain, the responsibility is entirely mine. They did their best for me. If I still did not learn, how can anyone blame them?

I had been writing this book based mainly on the experience gained from field journalism. Dr. (Mr.) Satya Srivastava, a psychologist who has gone deep into the subject, and Mr. Ashok Kumar, an Industrial Engineer with SAIL, helped by motivating me to study the psychological aspect of it. The result was two chapters, *Conceptual Support* and *The Smile and Advanced Journalism.*

Lastly, the hidden hand. The study had been going on for years. Many parts had been written. Yet, the habits of a lifetime die hard and things somehow do not come to fruition for a journalist without a deadline.

This spur was provided by Prof. M.R. Dua. Without my knowledge he indicated to the distinguished publisher, Mr. Narendra Kumar, who is bringing out this book that I had something valuable to say. The publisher, whose professional approach I have learnt to admire, went after me with letters, personal meetings and phone calls and made me complete the manuscript. My thanks to both Prof. Dua and Mr. Narendra Kumar.

Adarsh Kumar Varma

Preface to the Second Edition

Latest Developments

I had expected a polarised reaction to this book, and this is what happened. Some, mainly old time journalism teachers who had done years of teaching but only a limited amount of field work, seemed to think: "I have churned out so many batches of journalists, and here he comes saying there is something more to give to my students. What nonsense!"

At the other pole were veteran editors and field workers like Prem Bhatia, S.Nihal Singh, Vinod Mehta and MV Kamath who thought highly of the idea. They particularly applauded the idea of likening editorship to generalship and the practices of reporting and subediting to the work of the jawan, valuable and even vital as it is.

The success of the book has ended the dichotomy. It was published and sold out, then reprinted and again sold out, and now comes the second edition. Several universities now give glimpses of Advanced Journalism to their students, and some more than a few glimpses.

In this edition the concept of the new discipline has been further enlarged and explained. The chapters *Who Does What, Two Front Pages* and *Beginning and Flowering* explain how the concept germinated, took root and flowered. The fruits are before us in the form of our vastly transformed newspapers.

The first edition elaborated the concept by giving 7 case studies. The second has added two more, including one entitled *MID-DAY Sunshine*. This is a portentous development in Advanced Journalism. There was, for thousands of years, no newspaper reading habit because there was no newspaper. Then developed the newspaper reading habit and later the addiction to the morning daily. *MID-DAY* has established the new phenomenon of lunch time addiction. It is still confined to Mumbai where one more lunch time daily has sprouted in the shape of *The Afternoon Despatch and Courier*. The addiction is bound to spread as other metropolises develop to the size of the gargantuan Mumbai and as work culture gets globalised. Who knows, some day another Khalid Ansari may dream of a dinner time addiction, though there will be fierce competition from dinner time TV.

I have left the two chapters dealing with lessons from the case studies largely untouched. This is because the editing and public relations skills I envisaged for 2000 A.D. are still developing and in time will acquire newer dimensions. As I said in the first edition, the study continues and new ideas are emerging. These will be dealt with in the third edition, or maybe in another book.

Adarsh Kumar Varma

Preface

Why Advanced Journalism

The first two paragraphs of this book explain what Advanced Journalism is. The reader would, however, like to know when and how it dawned on me that it is a qualitatively different discipline from the bunch of skills which are collectively called Journalism.

It is rarely that journalists find time in the rough and tumble of daily working to pause and ponder about the complete Communication Package. Each reporter goes about cultivating the sources in his beat, getting news out of them and catching deadlines. Each subeditor is riveted to the news stories he is editing, trying to find headlines, squeezing his brain about the featuring and the illustrations and, again, catching deadlines. At the junior level most subeditors and reporters think one has to earn enough "seniority" to move up and then start barking orders to people junior to him.

For the three decades that I was a wholetime journalist these thoughts occurred to me. I wondered why it was that some newspapers and magazines were more popular, some less, some not at all.

Certain specific instances sent the brain ticking. In the early sixties a number of subeditors and reporters joined the *Statesman's* Delhi edition. Among them were some from the *Hindusthan Standard's* Delhi edition which had closed down. Started by the thriving *Ananda Bazar Patrika* Group, the *Hindusthan Standard,* first in Calcutta and then in Delhi also, was an attempt to muscle in on the *Statesman's* circulation and advertising in these two metropolises.

Why did the attempt fail after millions of rupees had been sunk in the venture? I worked in the *Statesman* with those who had come from the *Hindusthan Standard.* Charlie Bannerji was painstaking, productive, meticulous, sometimes brilliant. S. Guru Dev was a great headline man with a natural gift for the language. With them and other such men, one could work wonders.

Two decades later, the *Ananda Bazar* group decided to have another fling. It recruited talented people and spent money lavishly. This time the name of the paper was the *Telegraph.* It succeeded where the *Hindusthan Standard* had failed. The only difference I could think of was the higher direction. The Communication Package and the strategy devised, and most of all the man or men who did the devising, must have made the difference. The quality of higher direction available at the *Statesman* must also have mattered.

Another instance. The magazine boom is a very recent phenomenon. The fifties had the venerable *Illustrated Weekly of India,* which thrived on its pictures, its non-political stuff and its King's (Queen's) English. *Filmfare* started with a big splash of colour and was successful. Baburao Patel's *Filmindia* closed down. The *Hindu's Sport and Pastime* was wound up. It was said that India was not fertile ground for magazines, specially for specialist periodicals.

Within a few years Khalid Ansari, having inherited the Urdu daily *Inquilab,* launched *Sportsweek* which became the rage of middle class sports-loving households. *Junior Statesman* (later JS) became the heart-throb of adolescents. *Sportsweek's* success inspired others to launch similar sports magazines—*Sportsworld* and *Sportstar.* Surprise of surprises, one of them is owned by the group which had closed down *Sport and Pastime* only a few years earlier!

There were many, many such instances. In the fifties, I distinctly remember, the "Commerce" page was considered the dumping ground for journalists who could not prove themselves in other fields. The page itself was considered almost like a bitter pill, to be swallowed as a matter of necessity. It contained the quotations of the Bombay and Calcutta, and if possible Madras, stock exchanges, a short intro to explain the share price movements, commodity and bullion rates, and that's all. I have seen Chief Subs frequently raiding the "Commerce" page to accommodate the overflow of political and other news when they were hard up for space.

The "Commerce" page has now graduated to the multi-page Business section. Let anyone try to raid it today! Not only that, there are a number of financial dailies, and they are among the most prized and costly.

I kept wondering about these things during those three decades. During the last 10 years or so of my work as a full-time journalist I had responsibility for and occasion to devise, remodel or refashion the Communication Packages of a number of publications, dailies and weeklies. I learnt to ask myself the question: "Why should anyone want to buy/read my daily/weekly? Why would anyone want to switch over from the daily/weekly he is reading to my daily/weekly?"

When I joined the Indian Institute of Mass Communication in 1988 as a Consultant, I had for the first time enough of leisure to give deep thought to these questions and find the answers.

I discovered that trite sayings like "India is not fertile ground for periodicals" or "there is no scope for specialist (sport, business) publications" are frequently mouthed by defeated men, or by men who are mentally not keeping pace with the fast changing times. (No offence meant; we all fall behind the times at some time or the other in life).

Looking at the horizon beyond journalism, I found that in many fields the difference between the basic and advanced trades had already been recognised and acted upon. An example which came immediately to mind was that of the armed forces. All members of the army are fighters, but some are jawans and some Generals! Some jawans rise up to Generals. Example: Field Marshal Sir William Slim. Most officers start as second-lieutenant. Some retire as captain, some as major, some as colonel and so on. At every stage there is a process of selection. It is not as if the person who goes up to colonel is inferior to the one who rises to be a General. He may be an excellent and brave officer, leading from the front and setting an example. But those whose job it is to make the selection may discover that he does not have in adequate measure those qualities which are required for the trade of generalship. Or that others have these qualities in a more abundant measure. Those who are considered to have these qualities in adequate measure are trained into generalship.

This led to the realisation that Advanced Journalism is a different trade, even though it builds on the basic skills of journalism. Assuming that there are 40,000 journalists in India, only a few hundred or a thousand will ever become Editors. Those who will not become Editors include excellent reporters, subeditors, Chief Reporters, Chief Subeditors, Staff and Special Correspondents, Deputy News Editors and News Editors. Yet they may be lacking some of those qualities, or may be having them in an inadequate measure, which make an Editor.

I have tried to conceptualise the whole thing in the years since 1988. Two years ago, the Director, the faculty and then the Academic Council of the Indian Institute of Mass Communication included Advanced Journalism as a distinct segment in the Post-Graduate Diploma Course in Journalism (details in the chapter *The Beginning Of It*). Other journalism schools are also realising the importance of it. Some of them, including Banaras Hindu University and Delhi University, have been inviting me to give their Bachelors and Masters students a glimpse of the new discipline.

This book is divided into three broad sections. First, there are chapters which delineate the area of Advanced Journalism and try to relate it to the theories of management and leadership. There are then a number of case studies. They take up one case after another and give specific instances of what editorial touches and decisions made for success, where—and what failed. The cases studied—or, to be more precise, some aspects of which were studied—relate to the *Statesman,* the *United News of India,* the *Times of India,* the *Telegraph,* the *People* and Lucknow's the *Pioneer,* among others. There are also references to specific instances of Advanced Journalism at work in other papers like the *National Herald.*

The last two chapters look towards the future. I discovered that in Advanced Journalism as in no other trade the smile—and variants of it—plays a huge part. How, and why, the smile works is the subject of one of these chapters. The last chapter tries to visualise, based on decades of experience and observation, in which direction Advanced Journalism is likely to move in the 21st century.

This study is now dedicated to the reader, both lay and professional, and both to students of journalism and Advanced Journalism and to practitioners of these trades. In any case I maintain that all journalists have to continue to remain students throughout their lives. Anyone who neglects this part of the trade falls by the wayside, and in any case can never graduate to be a successful practitioner of Advanced Journalism.

One last word. Though the results of conceptualisation are being presented in this book, the study itself continues. I have the gut feeling, based on what I have studied so far and am continuing to study even now, that some more very interesting concepts will emerge. They will be incorporated in the next edition of this study, or maybe in another book.

That's all for now.

Adarsh Kumar Varma

Contents

New Discipline

Case Studies

Lessons from Case Studies

NEW DISCIPLINE

CHAPTER I

Dimensions of Advanced Journalism

Soldiers do the fighting but wars are won or lost by Generals. Likewise, reporters and subeditors write and process the news reports but it is called the Editor's paper, or a particular Chief Sub's edition.

The trade practised by Editors, and partially by News Editors, Chiefs of Bureau, etc., is Advanced Journalism.

Time was when kings and princes and tribal heads led their men into battle. But, for every Alexander who was both a prince and a great General, there were hundreds of princes who proved to be poor generals. Humayun was defeated and deposed by Sher Khan, who was far ahead in generalship. It was thus that Akbar, who was smart as a king, chose Raja Mansingh and other men naturally gifted in generalship to command his legions.

It was left to Europe to discover that waiting to spot people having a natural gift for generalship can be risky and sometimes unproductive. The best way to get competent generals who are to command armies in battle is to train them.

How Training Helps

There is no dispute that a man with the natural gifts of an Alexander or a Napoleon will prove superior to a man of average natural gifts trained in generalship. Likewise, a journalist of average gifts is unlikely, even with training in journalism, to match a natural Editor like M.J. Akbar (though Akbar too had training under Khushwant Singh). But a reporter or subeditor trained in Advanced Journalism is likely to prove at the very least a competent Chief Reporter/Chief Sub/ News Editor/Editor. If he has talent above the average, he may turn out to be a brilliant Chief Reporter/Chief Sub/News Editor/Editor.

Developed from an Extension Lecture delivered by the author to journalism teachers from all over India at the University Grants Commission's Academic Staff College at B.H.U. in 1991.

What does Advanced Journalism consist of? Whether it is a daily, a periodical, radio or TV, it is meant to deliver to its audience a Communication Package at a fixed time. The sources of news (including illustrations of all kinds) and comment (including cartoons) are unlimited. All news agencies keep ticking away almost round the clock delivering news collected by their reporters. The daily, the periodical, radio and TV have, additionally, their own staff to bring in news stories, There are speeches, seminars, declarations, events, parliaments, assemblies, riots, wars, famines, floods, good and bad deeds—the world is full of news waiting to be reported. There are also any number of writers, commentators, analysts, cartoonists and others ready to churn out their comment stuff when commissioned.

Constraint of Space

No Communication Package can accommodate all of these things. The daily newspaper has the constraint of space and so have the periodicals. The number of pages cannot be increased to accommodate everything that comes. Similarly, every radio or TV programme has a time constraint—each news bulletin, current affairs programme, or comment slot has a fixed time limit which cannot be exceeded.

This is where Advanced Journalism comes in. Whoever devises the Communication Package for a particular audience—the particular edition of a newspaper or the news bulletin to be broadcast at a particular time for a particular audience—has to pick and choose. He must not only choose particular news items to be used, discarding the rest, but decide which is to be used at what length within the space or time available.

Not only this, he must decide which item, as edited, gets which priority.

Newspaper readers know from experience, and Subeditors/Chief Subs/News Editors know from practice, that Page 1 mostly consists of spot stories of the greatest importance. However, most dailies make an effort to squeeze in a human interest story, a local crime or other striking story, or a sports or commerce story on Page 1 to cater to the interests of specialist readers who may have an inordinate interest in local/crime/sports/commerce news.

This is Advanced Journalism at the level of whoever produces the edition of a newspaper, which in a daily means the Chief Sub and in radio/TV means the News Editor.

But Advanced Journalism is not merely Chief Subbing. The Chief Sub's level is but one at which this trade is practised. As we have seen, the Chief Sub decides what is to go into his particular edition and what can wait (or need not go) depending upon the audience his particular edition is serving and the space available. The Chief Reporter, likewise, has to decide early in the morning which news events to cover and at what length, depending on the number of reporters he has, and which can be left to news agencies to tackle.

At the level of Special Correspondents who are accredited to the State or Central Government and whose job it is to report news emanating from the Government, it is the Chief of Bureau who decides which person is to do what, how much attention is deserved by a particular news development and how much space can be given to a particular news item. Of course, both the Chief Reporter and the Chief of Bureau take their decisions in consultation with the particular reporter/Special Correspondent who is to do the actual reporting. But it must be clearly understood that all the big "yeses" and "nos" have to come from the Chief Reporter or the Chief of Bureau.

There are other levels apart from those of the Chief of Bureau or the Chief Reporter at which the trade of Advanced Journalism is practised. Take the instance of the subeditor. He may be commissioned by the Chief Sub to tackle the many stories connected with the Gulf war. It may be indicated to him that the Gulf war would take as much as a third of Page 1, plus two whole pages inside. This having been decided, he has to pick and choose which stories are to go on Page 1 and which on inside pages, and at how much length, with that featuring, with which maps or illustrations, etc.

Final Decision

Of course he works in consultation with the Chief Sub of the particular edition and in accordance with the instructions left by the News Editor. If he disagrees with any of the instructions or directives, he is entitled to thrash it out with his Chief Sub or with the News Editor. Or, if a particular instruction has been left by the Editor, he may telephone the Editor and thrash out the matter with him. But the final decision, it must be understood, is of the man who is in charge of that particular edition. Implied in this is the understanding that, while the Chief Sub at night can overrule even the Editor, his edition will be evaluated by the News

Editor/Editor next morning and he can either be praised for his decisions or hauled over the coals.

Here is an example from my personal experience. The day in 1977 when the Janata party, newly created by merging all the major non-Congress parties except the communists, launched its election compaign, I was the Chief Sub in charge of the main edition of the Delhi *Statesman* at night. The major speakers at the Janata election campaign meeting at Delhi's Ramlila Grounds were Morarji Desai and Atal Behari Vajpayee. Such meetings were then routinely covered by staff reporters. But when I came to work at 7.30 p.m., I found a note from the Resident Editor, S. Sahay, with a supporting note from the News Editor, R.N. Sharma, advising me that instead of a staff reporter a senior Special Correspondent (called Special Representative in the *Statesman*) named D.P. Kumar had been detailed to cover the event. There was a further request to carry as much as possible of Kumar's report.

Detailed Coverage

Kumar, who rose by 1991 to be the Resident Editor of the *Statesman* in Delhi, is known for his detailed, ball-by-ball coverage of anything that he is assigned to report. He is also known for his accuracy to the last detail. Furthermore, Kumar writes in such a way that it is difficult to cut his report from the middle, so intertwined each paragraph is with the one preceding it and the one following it. Still further, I knew from experience that Kumar was a late starter.

Sure enough, as the meeting ended after 8 p.m., Kumar came to office about 9.30 p.m., took his time framing his report, and started sending the takes one by one not before 11 p.m. Having seen the Editor's instructions and knowing from radio news what Desai and Vajpayee had said, I was clear in my mind that it was the obvious lead story for Page 1 and would be long. I had therefore restricted other news items to manageable lengths and reserved the lead slot on Page 1 and a sizable chunk on Page 7 to take the turn.

Kumar wrote on and on, leaving no detail out, and the last page of his typed report came at about 1.30 a.m., a bare half an hour before lock-up time. I had never taken a single story at such length in any edition of any newspaper I had worked for, barring Jawaharlal Nehru's press conferences, which were reported almost verbatim in the *National Herald,* Lucknow, where I had been a Chief Sub until March 1964.

I therefore grumbled that it was an error of judgement on the part of the Resident Editor to ask for the whole of Kumar's report to be used. The subeditor handling the story, R. M. Kala, who is now (1993) a Deputy News Editor, grumbled even more. Next morning, it transpired, the *Statesman* report on the launching of the Janata campaign was the talk of the town. No other paper had covered it in such detail—and all readers seemed interested in all the nuances of the story. Sahay was proved right and I wrong.

I cite this instance to stress two points—first, that Advanced Journalism is practised at various levels and, second, that the decision taken by practitioners of the trade can have a vital bearing on the readability and readership, and hence credibility, of the paper. Different opposition in the editorial department of a newspaper have proportions of basic skills (like subbing and reporting) and Advanced Journalism. When a subeditor or reporter carries out instructions given by his seniors by using his skills, it is not Advanced Journalism, but when he finds he has no instructions, or instructions which are demonstrably inadequate or very wrong on how to handle a news story, and he uses his discretion, he practises Advanced Journalism.

Assume that a reporter is asked to cover a crime story as a routine—giving it one or two paragraphs or tucking it away in crime briefs. Consulting the police he smells a major crime, visits the spot and decides to treat it as a major story to be investigated and reported at length. His decision amounts to practising the trade of Advanced Journalism, for he is materially modifying the Communication Package by giving a 10-paragraph news story plus a picture or two where only one paragraph had been provided for.

Different Proportions

In the working of the junior reporter or junior subeditor, the element of basic journalism—which means the skills he has been taught—is preponderant, with Advanced Journalism forming a small part of his work. As he grows senior, he progressively gets greater discretion in deciding on the probable place of a news story in the Communication Package. At the level of the Chief Reporter or Chief Sub, the element of Advanced Journalism becomes very sizeable—and it goes on increasing as one goes further up.

Apart from quantity, the quality of the exercise of the powers of Advanced Journalism differs for each functionary. Here is a brief narration of the kind, extent and quality of Advanced Journalism practised by various functionaries in a newspaper.

The Editor devises the Communication Package to be given to the reader day after day. He may decide in consultation with various departments (Advertisement, Circulation, the Press, etc.) to have a 12-pager on weekdays and a 16-pager on Sunday. He may also apportion, say, two pages to local news in place of the customary one and so on and so forth. The job of deciding the character of each segment (local, sports, etc.) of the paper is also his. But he may delegate this responsibility to the person/persons handling a particular segment.

A few examples will make things clearer. Some 35 years ago Johnson was the Editor of the *Statesman.* He entrusted the job of giving a new thrust to the local page to his News Editor (Delhi) named James Cowley. The *Statesman* those days was carrying a local feature on top of Page 3 everyday. But since most of the staff reporters, who by and large contributed the local features, had to be given the weekly off on Sunday, the feature article for Monday morning was a perpetual headache. On the other hand, short human interest stories tended to be crowded out or cut out of shape on most days. Cowley asked the reporters and other journalists (including himself) to write factual human interest stories, which were not hard news, for a new weekly feature called "New Delhi Note Book". This was to be carried every Monday. He himself edited them to give them a consistent style.

Standard Monday Feature

Ever since then the *New Delhi Note Book* has become the standard local page feature every Monday morning. Not only this, every other English language paper in Delhi has emulated the *Statesman* by having a similar contributory feature every Monday morning.

The second example concerns the *Indian Express.* Some time in the 1950s, when the *Indian Express* was not catching on in Delhi, its then Editor thought of using sport as a booster. He appointed Vernon Ram his Sports Editor and the two of them worked out the following package:

1. The sport segment was transferred to the back page, something which no newspaper did those days. The idea was to make it more

visible to the reader who, if the sports page was interesting and spicy enough, would be tempted to buy the paper.

2. They decided that all sports news should be set indented and the column rules should be abolished. This made for a contrast between the grey matter of the text and the white between the columns, making for greater visual appeal.
3. It was decided to make the sports page more spicy, with action pictures, exclusive news items and a daily commentative column called "Ringside Seat" by Vernon Ram.

The sports package was such a fabulous success that the Delhi edition of the *Indian Express* took off and the need to price the paper lower than its rivals was obviated. On days when the *Express* lacked exclusive sports news items, readers were tempted to buy the paper just the same for the sake of reading about the doings and misdoings of various sports personalities, including players and officials, in "Ringside Seat" and other columns and news items/features.

Third Example

The third example of Advanced Journalism at the level of the Editor concerns Arun Shourie's reign as Editor of the *Indian Express.* Before Shourie (first as Executive Editor and then as Editor), the *Indian Express* tried to be "balanced" in the way every other paper in Delhi tried. Shourie dropped all such pretensions. His view of journalism is to arrive at what he perceives to be the truth without trying to "balance" the truth he has discovered with rival truths. This is because, as he says, "the truth concerns us all". Also because he believes there is only one truth in a specific situation, not many.

Shourie's supporters insist it is not a quest for an increased circulation. If the *Indian Express* picked up circulation, it was a by-product, according to this school of thought.

Shourie's critics, like his admirers, are many. Some feel he goes only selectively after the truth as he perceives it. Others feel he gives all the weight to his perception of the truth and none at all to the perceptions of others. Still others say that to be so deadly sure about what he perceives to be the truth is not good journalism, particularly in situations in which he does not or cannot elicit the versions of those who are materially affected by what his paper publishes. But, then, it can be argued that everyone depends upon his own perception of the truth.

At the News Editor's level, the general character of the Communication Package is fixed. He cannot change it. Indeed, he must not. I have given above the example of how a News Editor invented a collective weekly column to fulfil a felt need. But that was a once-for-all effort.

Everyday the News Editor must arrange for all the regular features which have been provided for in the original Communication package devised by the Editor. He must also ensure that the channels of news flow, including news agencies, reporters, Special Correspondents, and outstation and foreign correspondents, remain unclogged. He visualises how much space would be needed for news and features and arranges with the advertisement and administrative departments to ensure that that amount of space is available.

Grand Design

Another job of the News Editor is to chart a Grand Design for the day. Which features are to start from which edition, which Chief Sub and his team are to handle which edition, contingency planning for all editions of the day like holding in reserve a few features and/or pictures of various sizes and belonging to various segments—these are part of his daily job.

One important duty of the News Editor of which non-journalists are unaware is to maintain the character of the Communication Package. As stated earlier, every daily specialises in something or the other. This specialisation is like its face; it must not and cannot be changed. I remember that in the fifties and sixties, the *Statesman's* Delhi edition studiously cultivated the image of an exclusive elitist paper. It would, of course, adequately cover all the news that broke. But, apart from this, it would try to be as different from its contemporaries in Delhi as possible. There were four rules of the thumb:

1. It would go after its own exclusive news, which included both political and human interest stories, and make a big a splash of them with bold featuring, pictures, sketches, etc., regardless of what others did.
2. It would studiously keep off other papers' exclusive stories. That is, if a contemporary had an exclusive story one day, every other paper tried sheepishly to report it from a different angle next day—each one except the *Statesman*. The *Statesman* would try to follow up the news leads provided by its contemporaries' exclusives, but

if the leads yielded nothing, reporters, Special Correspondents and subeditors were barred from using a rehash of a contemporary's exclusive, even if it came via a news agency.

3. If the News Editor or a Chief Sub or subeditor made an error of judgement and did not use a story one day, they might be taken to task for it but were debarred from using the story next day. The image projected for the reader was that "we did not miss it, we left it out because it's not newsy enough for the *Statesman*."
4. The make-up and proof-reading must be impeccable. The effort was to conform to the dictum, "The *Statesman* doesn't use wrong spellings or wrong English". From this was derived the oft-repeated slogan: "Whatever the *Statesman* uses, that's English". It was, indeed, a bigger sin to carry wrong English or wrong spellings than to miss a news item!

Soon after I joined the *Statesman* in 1964, the News Editor went about making an assessment, with the help of his Chief Subeditors, whether I could take charge of editions. It did not seem to matter that I had been taking charge of editions in another paper for several years. The theory was that the *Statesman* Chief Sub (who takes charge of editions) has to be very special.

Talking Sessions

Having made the assessment, News Editor R.N. Sharma started having long talking sessions with me trying to impress upon me how very fastidious I had to be. There could be no mistakes of language or spelling, no widow lines, no clashing headlines, and all the other norms. One had to be particular to follow all these norms to be a *Statesman* Chief Sub. It was only when he was satisfied that I had absorbed it all that he allowed me to handle editions. In contrast, a colleague senior to me who had been given charge of editions was removed from charge after some years only because he was not fastidious enough.

I must say that R.N. Sharma was mighty successful as News Editor, though some of us (not including me) fumed why he made so much fuss over small matters. So long as he was there, the *Statesman* continued to enjoy its old reputation of spotless production. Among the readers and in the Newsrooms of other papers, if anyone had a doubt about a spelling, about the usage of a word or phrase, or about a name or designation, the standard practice was to pick up the *Statesman* and check. If the *Statesman* did it, it was the done thing, otherwise not.

While working for the *Statesman,* I was aware of this reputation. But when I moved to another paper in 1980, I saw how much it meant. All reporters, all subeditors, even the News Editor, the Assistant Editors and the Editor checked with the *Statesman* without diffidence. This is the measure of the success of R.N. Sharma and his predecessors as News Editor.

On the production side, the man next to the News Editor is the Chief Sub, though some papers have Deputy News Editors performing various specialised jobs. The Chief Sub is in charge of one edition or, when there is no edition in his shift, of the work of his shift which consists of preparing for the next edition. If in charge of an edition, he ensures that all the stories/features expected for it land, are processed, composed and put in their proper places in the paper. Contingency planning for his edition is also his job.

Role of Visualisation

If there is no edition in a Chief Sub's shift, his job is in some ways more difficult than if he were producing an edition. This is because while the man producing an edition works in close proximity to his lock-up time, which may be two, three or four hours away, the man working for an edition in the next shift has to visualise the situation as it would obtain five, six or more hours away when the edition is to be locked up. He must further visualise what his successor Chief Sub, in charge of the next edition, would think about the situation. Working for oneself is any day far easier than working for someone else.

The most important job of a Chief Sub, whether working for his own or his successor's edition, is to assess the relative importance of various news items, features and other inputs. He feeds them to the press in accordance with their importance. Naturally, he gets them prepared in proper sizes in accordance with their relative importance and the availability of space.

A corollary to this, but a vital one, is this: No Chief Sub worth his salt dare produce an edition which is less than "interesting" and "informative" to his readers. If he can make it "exciting", so much the better.

This is the dictate of the trade of Advanced Journalism. An insipid edition cannot be justified on the ground that—

A. The News Editor laid out only this fare for me, apart from the reports of the news agencies and reporters.

B. The newsfall was unexciting: or that nothing extraordinary happened in Delhi (or place of publication)/India/the rest of the world.

Indeed, one of the most important principles I have evolved while working at the desk or in reporting, and as News Editor, Assistant Editor, Deputy Editor and Editor in various papers, both dailies and weeklies, runs as follows:

There is no such thing as a dull day for news; there are only dull or bright Editors/News Editors/Chief Subs/Chief Reporters.

As a corollary to this, a Chief Sub in command of the early morning edition, which is the main edition of all newspapers, invariably assumes the powers of both the Editor/News Editor and the Manager as soon as these functionaries have done their stint and retired home. This is so whether it is laid down in writing or not. Specifically, he has the power to command the Chief of Bureau, the Special Correspondents, the Chief Reporter and his staff reporters to "produce or perish" if the newsfall is sparse and unexciting. If they do not deliver, it may be their fault but it is the Chief Sub's funeral. The reasons for such a peremptory prescription are two:

1. The production of a daily newspaper is, as the late K. Rama Rao was fond of saying, like a battleship being in action. There is a gold medal for the winner but no silver for the loser or bronze for anyone else.
2. The production of an interesting and informative Communication Package directly affects circulation which in turn affects advertisement revenue. Advertisement revenue being the life blood of a newspaper, a poor Communication Package produced day after day may prove fatal for a newspaper.

The difference between the functioning of a Chief Sub and the Editor/News Editor is as follows:

The Chief Sub's constituency is the world at the moment, the News Editor's the world this day and the Editor's the changing world.

In reporting, there are two broad categories. The Chief of Bureau marshals his team of Special Correspondents in such a way that the team can give maximum coverage to the activities, including shortcomings, of the Government. This includes invariably special and exclusive stories which he plans in consultation with his team.

The Chief Reporter similarly plans his city coverage in such a way that he and his team of reporters do not leave out any particular newsworthy area or development. At the same time, he must keep an eye on how interesting his team's coverage of the city is. If it threatens to be sparse and uninteresting to the reader, he and his team think up new ideas and put in a special effort.

It is said that a good reporter always has a news story up his sleeve. This is even more true of Chief Reporters. A good Chief Reporter is one whose team's coverage of the city and its developments is both adequate and interesting to the reader. If it is not interesting enough, he should have contingency plans to make it interesting.

Contingency planning is each Chief Reporter's professional secret. But here are some ideas. At one time in the early sixties News Editor C.S. Smith and Chief Photographer Capt. Arjun of the *Statesman* in Delhi thought of exploiting the enormous potential of the Delhi Zoo. If they visualised that nothing much was likely to happen in the city next day, they and Chief Reporter N. N. Rana detailed a team consisting of a photographer and a reporter to reach the Zoo early next morning. The result was a series of very interesting Zoo features week after week for four or five years. They would watch and click various animals at various times—getting up from sleep, having breakfast, reacting to those who came to the Zoo, having their siesta, and so on.

Another fruitful source of human interest stories is the large number of women's, children's, and other such citizens' groups. If a reporter, a Chief Reporter or a News Editor maintains contact with their active members, one can be sure of getting an interesting sob story or other human interest item from them whenever in need of providing liveliness to the city's news coverage.

Requisites of Advanced Journalism

The three major requisites of Advanced Journalism, thus, are:

1. **Visualization**—by the Editor of which group of people are the likely audience; of their tastes and needs commensurate with the public interest.

   Within the parameters set by the Editor, visualisation by the News Editor of the likely audience of particular editions, their tastes, needs and interests.

   Within the parameters set by the News Editor, visualization by the Chief Sub of the audience of his particular edition, their tastes, needs, interests, etc.

Example: If an edition is going to Nagpur, it is mandatory for the Chief Sub to play up any news and/or feature on the orange crop which is a major produce of the region.

2. **Product mix:** Each edition going, say, to Nagpur must be a perceptible advance on the last edition which went to that area. It should contain (a) news and features of the area and the region, and (b) national and international news and features of interest to the people of the region.
3. **Contingency planning:** While the News Editor does contingency planning for all editions of the day (including advance planning for the next day and the day after the next), the Chief Sub is responsible for his own contingency planning.

It is not good enough for the Chief Sub to say that since the matter was inadequate to fill up the space he pushed in a particular feature whose suitability was earlier indicated by the News Editor. He must ask himself whether the feature fits in at the place he is pushing it in. Is it a foreign feature being pushed into the national page? Is it outdated? Does it need updating or re-editing?

Deadline

In other words, the Chief Sub must keep reviewing the contingency plans handed him by the News Editor or those drawn up by himself, and keep adding to or modifying them in accordance with the developing situation. If the composing system is crippled by machinery failure and/or lack of operators, or if some expected stories/features/pictures do not materialise, he must have alternative arrangements ready.

Also, if there is a surplus he must know what to hold over, what to condense, what to leave out.

All journalism is deadline oriented. But it is the job primarily of the practitioner of Advanced Journalism to ensure that the deadline is maintained without sacrificing input or quality. This applies to all disciplines—reporting, editing at various levels, article writing, editorial writing, production of editions, etc. This can be stated in the following way:

All products of journalism are highly perishable. The best news item in the world, the best editorial, article or analysis, presented in the best way possible and edited with consummate skill, is wasted if given after the deadline. Its utility diminishes in proportion to the amount of time beyond the deadline used to deliver it up to the stage when it becomes useless.

It is not good enough for a Chief Reporter/reporter to say that his news source came late, or for the Chief Sub to say the reporter did not turn in his copy on time, the subeditor was slow or that the composing was behind time.

Indeed, there are many occasions when a newspaper is striken by lack of men or machines. Yet the paper must come out on time—and without compromising quality or content. I can recall many occasions in the *Statesman* when only six lino machines out of 16 were operational. There were two occasions within my personal experience when only a two-man editorial team, including the Chief Sub, produced the main edition though the usual strength of the main shift was six. On one occasion it was R. K. Mukker, who several years later retired as the Editor of the *Searchlight* of Patna, and myself. On the other, Yash Paul Narula, later News Editor of the *Statesman* and of the *Hindu* in Delhi, assisted me in producing the main edition. I feel proud that on both occasions the edition was full, clean and on time—no story missed and no aberrations showing. The readers could not have imagined on any of these two occasions that it was an edition produced by an editorial team reduced to a third of its normal strength for one reason or the other.

Similarly, when I was Resident Editor of *MID-DAY* (Delhi edition), there were several occasions when the photosetting system collapsed. But we always had contingency plans.

Standby arrangements had been made with commercial photosetting firms, so when the system failed we sent news stories and features in relay by taxi to the standby photosetting shops, brought the bromides back, and produced the paper on time—or almost. The next norm of Advanced Journalism thus is:

No casualty in men or machines can, or should, ever affect the production of a Communication Package—in time, quality or content.

CHAPTER II
Conceptual Support

Conceptual support for the discipline of Advanced Journalism is provided by the newly-emerged theory of management. Paul Hersey and Kenneth H. Blanchard, in their celebrated book *Management of Organisational Behaviour,* provide extensive evidence based on the theories of psychology and management, how the Top Management, the Middle Management and the Supervisory Management need conceptual, human and technical skills in different proportions.

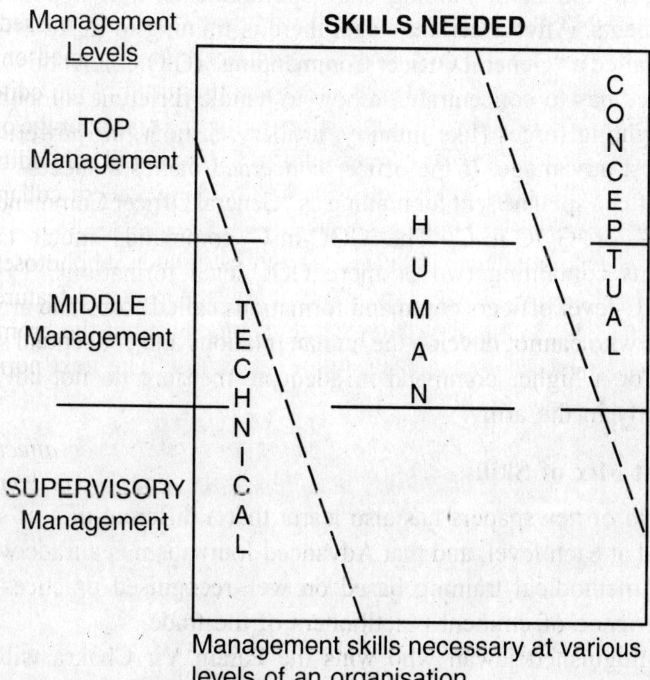

Management skills necessary at various levels of an organisation.

As the above figure shows, people at the Editor level need conceptual and human skills in preponderant proportions and technical skills in very small quantities. The Middle Management people, that is practitioners of Advanced Journalism at levels lower than the Editor, need a lot of human skill, a little less of but still substantial conceptual skill and more of technical skills than the top man. The Supervisory Management, that is people like Chief Reporter and Chief Sub, need mostly human and technical skills, with not much of conceptual skill.

As for the non-management level, most of the skills needed by, say, subeditors and reporters are technical and human. The conceptual skill needed is of a much lower order than in the case of the Chief Reporter or the Chief Sub.

G.O.C.s

Armies have learnt the hard way that each rung at which the trade of fighting wars is practised requires a different mix of skills. Consequently, there are different levels of training. There is training in the skills of wielding weapons, in holding staff appointments and in command appointments. After a certain stage, there is training to make officers what is called a "General Officer Commanding" (G.O.C.). At this level, the trainee has to concentrate on how to handle different components of the fighting forces (like infantry, artillery, armour, air power, etc.) to the best advantage. If the officer concerned makes a success of it, he may after a spell be sent for training as "General Officer Commanding-in-Chief" or GOC-in-C. The GOC-in-C commands much larger formations containing two or more GOC-level formations. Typical GOC-in-C-level officers command formations called corps and armies.

Those who cannot develop the human relations and conceptual skills needed for a higher command in adequate measure do not advance sufficiently in the army.

Different Mix of Skills

The world of newspapers has also learnt that a different mix of skills is needed at each level, and that Advanced Journalism is a trade which requires methodical training based on well-recognised practices and the experience of eminent practitioners of the trade.

A distinguished jawan who wins the Param Vir Chakra will not necessarily become an efficient Colonel, a competent Brigadier, or a

General who wins wars. A Preminder Singh Bhagat won the Victoria Cross while still at the bottom rung of the ladder. He went on after a succession of training courses over three decades to become Lieut-General Bhagat. But for every Lt. Bhagat who became a Lieut-General, there were dozens of winners of the Victoria Cross or the Param Vir Chakra who advanced only by two or three rungs.

Likewise, all distinguished reporters/subeditors do not necessarily become efficient or even competent News Editors or Editors. Most retire at the level of Chief Reporter, Deputy News Editor or Special Correspondent.

The Editor needs mostly conceptual and human relations skills. He should have, and usually has because he was probably a reporter/subeditor once, a lot of technical skills. But he stands or falls only depending upon whether he has conceptual and human relations skills of a high order. Even if he was a relatively ordinary reporter/subeditor, he can be a good Editor provided he has sharp and abundant conceptual and human relations skills.

The News Editor/Chief of Bureau falls in the Middle management category. He should have, most of all, a lot of human relations skill and sufficient conceptual skill. He should also have a fair amount of technical skill.

The Chief Sub/Chief Reporter falls into Supervisory Management category. Both should have a lot of technical and human relations skills and a little of conceptual skill.

So far, journalism has carried on without an awareness of this—just as in olden days kings and princes led armies into battle. Sometimes they did things well and sometimes messed things up.

Hence the need for full and unabashed training in and learning of Advanced Journalism. Naturally, such training can be imparted only by those with actual field experience of practising the trade, who have learnt the trade and developed it in various situations.

The biggest teacher of the trade is the daunting experience of taking part in the launching of newspapers or periodicals, or of editions of newspapers/periodicals with the main edition at another centre.

I learnt more about Advanced Journalism when I launched the Delhi editions of *MID-DAY* (daily) and *Current* (weekly), and also when I revived the *People* weekly (which had closed down some five months earlier) than during all my work as subeditor/reporter, Chief Sub, News

Editor, Assistant Editor, Deputy Editor and Editor in established papers (the *Pioneer,* the *Statesman,* the *National Herald,* etc.)

People who have been distinguished reporters/subeditors can teach reporting and subediting. But Advanced Journalism need not necessarily be their cup of tea.

The following figure shows how planning and motivating is primarily the responsibility of top and middle level practitioners of Advanced Journalism and how controlling and organising is primarily done by the Middle and Supervisory level journalists.

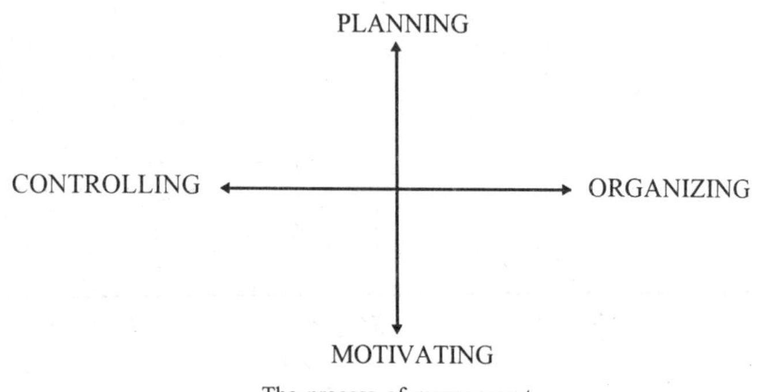

The process of management.

OBJECTIVITY: A GOD OR A BORE?

Journalism schools the world over teach the virtues of objectivity in reporting news. Here are the views of two Editors on objectivity, one Indian, the other American.

Girilal Jain, the celebrated former Editor of the *Times of India,* writes in the book *Communication 2000 AD**: "Journalism is, by its very nature, partisan. This does not mean that we call objective journalism a hoax... A good journalist is by definition an objective journalist... . (But) clearly an objective journalist is not a value-free automaton... He is deeply committed to certain values. As such he is partisan in support of groups, parties and governments which, in his judgement, stand for those values and seek to promote them."

In America, Geneva Overholser, Editor of the *Des Moines Register,* says too many newspapers are too often "mincing around, hoping we won't offend anyone." Her diagnosis: "A big piece of why so much news copy today is boring as hell is this objectivity god."

*Edited by the author of this book.

CHAPTER III
Who Does What

The time from 1988, when I switched from full-blown field journalism to teaching the subject, was the period of incubation for Advanced Journalism. Apart from catching up on the reading and preparing the lectures there was time to ponder over some key questions.

Why are dailies different from each other each day? If, as the *New York Times* proclaims, one uses "all the news that's fit to print," then all the newspapers on any day should be alike. Granting that the featuring may differ from daily to daily—that is, the news which one paper has on Page 1 can be on an inside page in another—at least the total Communication Package should be the same in all the dailies.

Obviously, each daily must be having someone who decides which news item goes on which page and at what length, and with which and how big a headline. Further, each paper has some special features all its own. Some papers have a column named *Periscope on Pakistan* but others do not have it. The *Statesman* at one time carried two weekly features entitled *Gardening Notes* and *Motoring Notes* but its contemporaries did not have them. Obviously there must be someone who decides the kinds of features his daily would have. And since everyone cannot write on gardening or motoring, the person taking the decision would also decide who would write a particular daily, weekly, fortnightly or monthly feature, and whether the feature needed an illustration and, if yes, what kind and size of illustration and by whom.

At a communication workshop held at IIMC for army officers of the rank of Brigadier, I tried to explain the concept and impact of Advanced Journalism. The officers, however, seemed to hold on to the popular but inaccurate notion that journalism consisted only of reporting events, giving expert opinions on them, and editing what was written.

Since they were high-ranking army officers, an example from military matters seemed to me what the doctor ordered. Why was it,

I asked, that while jawans/naiks/captains did the fighting and many of them died during the 1971 war, the man who was called the liberator of Bangladesh was General Jagjit Singh Aurora, even though he did not so much as wield a gun? Pat came the reply from one of the brigadiers: "Because his job was to orchestrate the action, not to wield the gun." Likewise, the job of the reporters and subeditors is to collect and place the news in the Communication Package while the Editor orchestrates the action, I told them.

Here is an illustrative list of the priorities of the General and the jawan:

PRIORITIES

Generals	**Jawans**
– visualisation	– personal courge
– strategic and tactical awareness	– never-say-die spirit
– faith in the cause	– expertise in wielding his weapons
– ingenuity	– faith in commander's orders
– knowledge of the Grand Design and the objectives aimed at	– faith in the cause he is fighting for
– faith in commander's orders	– tactical awareness
– expertise in wielding weapons	– visualisation
– personal courage	

This is not an exhaustive list. One can add to the priorities of the General or of the jawan. One can have a different list of priorities for each. For instance, "expertise in wielding weapons" can be promoted one notch higher to second place in the jawan's priorities. But no one will surely put "personal courage" at the top of the General's priorities or at the bottom of the jawan's. The reason is that all armies take great pains to guard their generals, who are in any case generally well behind the lines where fighting takes place. Though hundreds on both sides died in the 1971 war and 93,000 Pakistani troops had to surrender, their commander, General Amir Abdullah Khan Niazi, was mever in any danger personally.

In contrast with generals, a jawan who does not have personal courage as the first priority would not last a minute in a battle. In fact, anyone whose motto is "safety first"would not join the army at all. The fact is, it was General (later Field Marshal) SHFJ Maneckshaw and

General Aurora who devised the strategy and General Aurora who fine-tuned it during implementation.

The story is told that when General Tikka Khan unleashed his legions in East Pakistan (now Bangladesh) and refugees poured into India, Mrs Gandhi consulted General Maneckshaw about using the Indian army. Maneckshaw's response was that if it was to be like 1965, with gains in some areas and losses in others, he could order the army to move against Tikka Khan's forces immediately. But it could be decisive only if a Grand Design was painstakingly prepared and appropriate weapons were procured and used.

During the first few days of the war I interviewed General Harbaksh Singh about the strategy which was advisable. He had commanded during the 1965 war "the largest army in battle in India's history", as he was fond of pointing out. His prescription was that General Aurora should make a dash to secure the crossing points of East Bengal's many rivers, which means the bridges and the points where the rivers were narrow. He lamented that General Aurora was not doing this.

General Maneckshaw, on the other hand, had employed another strategy. He had persuaded the Government to import hordes of amphibious PT-76 tanks and giant helicopters with night vision which could each ferry about two dozen fully armed troops per sortie.

Pakistan's General Niazi apparently believed that securing and fortifying the bridges and crossing points was vital.

General Maneckshaw and General Aurora simply bypassed these strongly held defences, fording the rivers with the PT-76 tanks and ferrying helicopter-borne troops behind the enemy lines. The Moynamati Cantonment's impregnable defences were bypassed by three giant helicopters ferrying fully-armed troops all night behind Moynamati's defenders. When morning broke the defenders found Indian troops not only facing them but also behind their lines.

This digression into military matters is meant to show how Advanced Journalism is like generalship, much as reporting and subediting are like the jawan's work. Visualisation of readership, the likely impact of the Communication Package devised and its potential for diffusion (that is, how far the impact will spread) are the beat of Editor. This can be explained by the following statement of likely priorities:

PRIORITIES

Editors

- Visualisation of the audience/ readership, their tastes, needs, preferences, allergies
- The impact of the Communications Package on those potentially part of audience/readership
- The degree of diffusion of package and of individual items within it

Subeditors/Reporters

- The need to catch deadlines, which item to take on which page at what length
- How to display the item to catch readers' attention
- How to illustrate item (picture graph/sketch, etc.)
- How to confine wordage within processing capability

As in the case of generals and jawans, this listing of priorities is illustrative and not exhaustive. The reporters and subeditors will be mostly concerned with filling up the space available with the reports and other inputs. They will be concerned with displaying the matter to the best advantage of the paper and with catching the deadline.

Editors will, on the other hand, be concerned with the following issues:

1. What kind of items to give to the readers.
2. Who can best produce the kind of items envisaged and at what price and how soon?

Reporters are one group of people who provide the inputs. There are, then, specialist writers, commentators, columnists, cartoonists, cartographers,etc., who also provide the input. The Chief Sub and the subeditors play a role after the input has been received. They plan the placing and the display and do the polishing and rounding off of rough edges of individual, and groups of, items. Finally they plan to achieve these objectives within the deadline.

In the chapter on *Nihal Singh's Emergency* is cited the "Jaipur flight missed" episode. The flight was missed because the Press Manager did not provide sufficient staff for the third night running. While one can use ingenuity to get printing started on time even if there is a slight delay in preparing the edition (the chapter on *Times of India Comes to Delhi* describes how this can be done), the norm is to ready the edition on time. This helps build up circulation figures. Circulation figures in turn are like Television's TRP ratings. If the TRP rating is high one can get much advertising. Similarly, consistently high circulation figures can enable a newspaper to keep its advertisement rate high, raking in revenue. High revenue is necessary because if there is shortage of money, fewer reporters and subeditors and production staff can be deployed than necessary. It may also lead to cutting down on news gathering costs including travelling, which leads in turn to poor production quality, which translates into low circulation.

The whole process is circular and each stage is interdependent with the others and can be depicted as follows:

Interdependence Graph

Quality production → High circulation

↓

More money for inputs

↓

More reporters, subeditors, production staff

↓

Good quantity and quality of news, features, etc.

↓

Quality production

It will be observed that whenever the quality and quantity of input (news, features, etc.) deteriorates, the effect is felt downstream throughout the chain. That is why there are good publications, indifferent publications and bad publications. And that is why there is an occasional death (the *Hindusthan Standard, Filmindia,* etc.) and the occasional rise of new publications (the *Telegraph*, the *Asian Age*. *Eenadu, Outlook,* etc.).

THEY ASKED FOR IT

During the Gulf war, American daily *Newsday* began a "Students' briefing page" to let young people know what the fuss was all about. The war ended, but so well received was it that *Newsday* has made it a permanent three-times-a-week feature.

CHAPTER IV

"Two Front Pages"

The last decade (1990-2000) of the past millenium has shown the need for, and the luxuriant fruits of, innovation. When Hiranmay Karlekar, who had been a colleague at the *Statesman,* migrated to the *Hindustan Times* as its Editor in 1975, he solicited suggestions from friends. I contributed several. One of them was "two front pages". That is, apart from the traditional front page which carries the latest and most important of the news, the last page of the daily issue which is equally visible to the reader should become a theme page made up in the Page 1 format—with a lead story, a second lead, illustrations, an anchor, etc.

The theme I suggested was "business". Those days dailies did not carry a whole business section, only what was called the "Commerce" page. The multi-page business section of today's major dailies was a later development, the work of the practitioners of Advanced Journalism.

An alternative to "business" which I suggested for the last page was news analysis-cum-features. This would give readers the background of the news and the perspective.

The suggestion did not find favour with the *Hindustan Times* then. Today every major daily has what is called the "Op Ed Page" (opposite edit page) which carries news analysis-cum-features

The "two front pages" idea has been brilliantly implemented by the *Indian Express* now. It consists of the main edition of usually 14 pages carrying the multi-page sports and business sections, sections carrying foreign and national news, an edit page and an Op Ed Page. There is, then, a daily pullout of 8 pages called *Express Newsline* carrying local and mofussil news, formatted exactly like the main edition – a front page complete with lead, second lead , anchor, etc.,two pages of news items which are important to readers but which could not make it to the front page, a local and mofussil sports page, a page full of TV programmes and birthday forecasts and a page focused on eating out, education, personalities, etc.

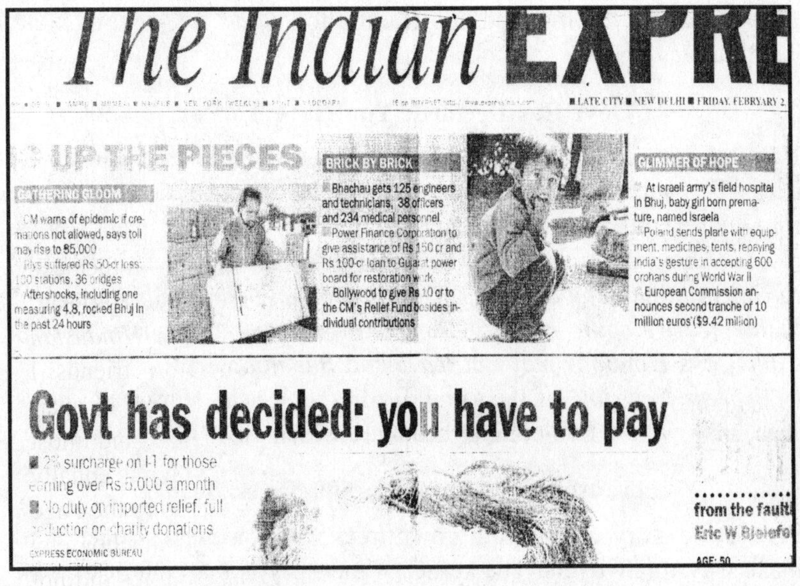

The Indian EXPRE

LATE CITY ■ NEW DELHI ■ FRIDAY, FEBRUARY 2,

UP THE PIECES

GATHERING GLOOM

CM warns of epidemic if cremations not allowed, says toll may rise to 85,000
Rlys suffered Rs 50-cr loss: 100 stations, 36 bridges
Aftershocks, including one measuring 4.8, rocked Bhuj in the past 24 hours

BRICK BY BRICK

Bhachau gets 125 engineers and technicians, 38 officers and 234 medical personnel
Power Finance Corporation to give assistance of Rs 150 cr and Rs 100-cr loan to Gujarat power board for restoration work
Bollywood to give Rs 10 cr to the CM's Relief Fund besides individual contributions

GLIMMER OF HOPE

At Israeli army's field hospital in Bhuj, baby girl born premature, named Israela
Poland sends plane with equipment, medicines, tents, repaying India's gesture in accepting 600 orphans during World War II
European Commission announces second tranche of 10 million euros ($9.42 million)

Govt has decided: you have to pay

■ 2% surcharge on I-T for those earning over Rs 5,000 a month
■ No duty on imported relief, full deduction on charity donations

EXPRESS ECONOMIC BUREAU

from the fault
Eric W Bjelefe
AGE: 50

ONE DAY, TWO FRONT PAGES

The Indian EXPRESS

Transplanting disaster: 500 trees dead

HC pulls u
for their w

EXPRESS NEWS SERVICE

Take the example of the *Indian Express* of February 2, 2001. The Page 1 lead in the main edition has the following five-column-wide headline:

Govt Has Decided: You Have To Pay

It is the story of the Union Cabinet decision to issue an ordinance to levy a 2% surcharge on income-tax to collect Rs 1,300 crores a year for Gujarat earthquake relief and rehabilitation. The other major stories also are about the quake—*Can Bhuj rise from the rubble*? *Meet Israela, tiny birth in the land of the dead,* and *Blood on their hands, Gujarat's builders are on the run,*etc. There are only two non-quake stories, *Court says Hindujas may not leave* and *Bus hijacked.*

Express Newsline of the same day has as lead, a New Delhi news item, also with a five-column headline, which is:

Transplanting Disaster: 500 Trees Dead

This is the story of 600 full-grown trees which were transplanted to make way for flyovers. The kernel of the story is that 500 of the 600 transplanted trees have died.

The second lead is a news item with the following thick three-column headline:

HC Pulls up Civic Bodies For their Wasted Efforts

It tells readers that the Delhi High Court has "expressed its displeasure over the sanitary conditions in the city...." The story further tells readers that the court has directed the Commissioner of Delhi Municipal Corporation, the New Delhi Municipal Council (NDMC) Chairman, Delhi Development Authority (DDA) Vice-Chairman and the General manager of the Northern Railway to appear before it to answer charges.

The reason for two front pages is that the audience today is far more awake than, say, 10 years ago. It has wider interests and much more thirst for information. There are about 100 television channels beaming all kinds of information to him compared to a few years ago when there was only Doordarshan. This is apart from radio beams from across the world.

To be fair, it was the Telugu language daily *Eenadu* of Ramoji Rao which pioneered this particular innovation. Apart from the mother edition giving all the main news, each district of Andhra has a separate pullout distributed with the paper giving local news.

If major newspapers are to survive the competition of satellite TV and local news sheets, they have to widen and deepen their appeal. This is what *Eenadu* and the *Indian Express* have done.

For years after I started out in journalism, how to prepare *kathi* and *shami kebab* and uncommon dishes and where to get the best of them and at what prices were not considered newsworthy enough. Today, tell me of any major newspaper which does not carry such recipes from well-known chefs and the names of places where these goodies can be got, and at what price.

Journalism, like most other trades, is growing. Indeed, man himself has grown from the time when he roamed about naked and grew long hair and whiskers. Someone must have then thought that growing a moustache was enough to distinguish man from woman at first sight. Later realisation dawned that even the moustache was not necessary, and the clean shaven male was born.

In news, as in everything else, perception is reality, as Dr Yadava is fond of emphasizing. *Eating Out* was discovered by *Busybee* Behram Contractor (alas, now dead) in Bombay (now Mumbai). Similarly, an exhibition of Lucknow's *chikan* clothes and a Mexican food festival were not news at one time. Now newspapers go to great lengths, deploying specialists as reporters and spending lavishly to cover such events.

Lastly comes the first law enunciated in *The 22 Immutable Laws of Marketing,* a best seller written by Al Rais and Jack Trout. The authors call it *The Law of Leadership* and it states:

It is better to be first than it is better to be better.

The authors really are emphasising the case for innovation. The *Indian Express* has, with its daily pullout *Express Newsline,* scored over its contemporaries in the two-front-pages race.

The contemporaries have, wisely, refused to imitate the *Express.* Instead they have made their own innovations. Apart from their own daily pullouts named *Delhi Times* and *HT City* which though having deceptively misleading names carry entirely different material, they give to the reader pullouts named *West Delhi Plus* and *West Delhi Live.* These try to penetrate different colonies in their areas reporting on schools, clubs and sanitation and traffic problems. There are other innovations like focusing on specific areas of life, like *HT estates* of the *Hindustan Times* and *Education Times* and *Government Business* of the *Times of India.*

All these are deeds of Advanced Journalism. Some may not click, but that is no reason to give up visualising readers' needs and interests and amending and adjusting the Communication Package accordingly. For, if someone had not visualised the need for clothing, someone else had not visualised growing crops for food, and a third person had not invented the wheel, we would still be living in the stone age—naked, hunting and gathering forest produce for food, and taking shelter in caves and under trees.

THE BUDDHA MIGRATION

As the Taliban started demolishing the mighty Buddha statues in Bamiyan, the Indian Ambassador in Moscow, Mr Satinder Kumar Lamba, attended a function celebrating Mikhail Gorbachov's 70th birthday and presented him a stone Buddha statue. Five days later Kirghizistan unveiled a 1,500-year-old Buddha statue which had been found by archaeologists 35 years ago.

Moral: If you want to have a future, value your past.

CHAPTER V

Beginning and Flowering

Though the Indian Institute of Mass Communication (IIMC), Delhi, runs at least three full-time courses in journalism, in 1988 its faculty had no one who had reached the level of Editor in any publication. When I joined it, I was asked to take classes on such topics as "What the Editor expects from a reporter" and "What the Editor expects from a subeditor". And naturally, since I had been the Editor of two publications, the *Pioneer* daily and the *People* weekly. Not only this, I was, concurrently with teaching, editing IIMC's scholarly research journal, *Communicator.*

What did I expect reporters and subeditors in the *Pioneer* and the *People* to do? What was I expecting contributors to *Communicator* to write?

Memories, thoughts and ideas came flooding to the mind. I kept noting them down. I also noted down what I had done to remodel, update and improve the *Pioneer's* and the *People's* Communication Packages in Lucknow. Further, since I had devised the Communication Package of the *Pioneer's* Delhi edition, I noted how it differed from the menu which had been so successful in Lucknow.

I taught the students from these notes and it was a great hit with them. They learnt not only how to implement a given Communication Package but how to devise a new one or remodel an old one. They also learnt that the Communication Package which was a hit in Lucknow did not necessarily have to be a hit in Delhi, for the audience was different in Delhi from the audience in Lucknow.

For a very special reason, I kept sending copies of these notes to IIMC's Director, Dr J.S. Yadava. Though three decades old in field work, I was new to journalism teaching and was not too sure whether the things I was giving to the students would be appreciated by the Institute, though the students seemed to be happy enough.

For some weeks there was no response from Dr Yadava. I wasn't sure whether he was reading and appreciating them or consigning them to the waste paper basket.

Then it happened. It was my practice to come to work and be operational bang on time, as I had learnt to do during my time in field journalism.

One day at about 9-25 a.m., as I was locking my car someone patted my back. It was Dr Yadava, who too made it a point to come on time. "I have been reading your notes," he said. "Come with me."

Dr. J. S. Yadava

He led me to his office and brought out from his drawer a file containing the notes, adding: "These are valuable."

I kept sending copies of such notes to him, and apparently he kept filing them. Then, at one faculty meeting, he broached the subject, asking me to explain what I wanted aspiring journalists to learn.

In my opinion, I told the assembled professors, training young people to become subeditors and reporters was laudable but not enough. We must also tell them of the job to be done after two or three years as a subeditor or reporter. I called it "higher journalism."

The faculty heard me with rapt attention. No one raised an objection. There were, in fact, some helpful suggestions. The new segment to be taught was approved, the only difference being that instead of "higher journalism" it was called "advanced journalism" on Dr Yadava's suggestion.

The next step was to get it approved by the Academic Council, and this was done. In time Dr Yadava got so taken in by the idea that he suggested running courses in Advanced Journalism for mid-career professionals. He also wanted the News Agency Journalism course, which is meant for mid-career journalists from non-aligned countries, to be designated as the Advanced Journalism course. IIMC wrote to the Government suggesting the change, since it is a Government-sponsored course. But for its own reasons—something to do with international agreements entered many years earlier—the Government did not permit the change.

Undeterred, I continued to include the new input in what I taught.

In 1993, it was decided rather suddenly to open a new campus of IIMC in a place called Dhenkanal in Orissa. Most faculty members were unwilling to move from Delhi and no one who had a stake in the profession of teaching journalism seemed willing to go to Dhenkanal, which is a largely tribal district town with no newspaper, daily or periodical, or radio or other media organisation. One faculty member said Dhenkanal would be a punishment posting. If the Director disliked someone he would be sent to Dhenkanal. Another professor, a Doubting Thomas, obviously thinking he was more worldly wise than others, said if the students in Dhenkanal, who he assumed would be backward compared to the Delhi students, trudged Delhi and Mumbai streets for three years not getting a job what reputation would I have?

This made my professional pride well up. For more than a decade before joining IIMC I had been in a position to guide the raw young people who joined the *Statesman,* the *Pioneer,* the *National Herald* and *MID-DAY,* and all of them had made good. How could the Dhenkanal campus students, who would be admitted as in Delhi on the basis of an all-India test, fail to become good journalists? I told the Doubting Thomas: "If I train them, they *will* become journalists." I agreed to go to Dhenkanal.

A little before the Dhenkanal project had come up, Dr Yadava, as besotted as me with the idea of Advanced Journalism, had suggested that I prepare a syllabus for a full course in Advanced Journalism and sound senior professionals, specially well-known editors, about it. I prepared a draft syllabus and met and wrote to two dozen seniors, who all replied. They all approved of the idea and suggested various changes in the syllabus, mainly additions. I revised the syllabus and sent copies back to them. Based on the responses, I prepared a third and a fourth revised syllabus incorporating the suggestions as they came. The idea was that when a broad agreement was reached, IIMC would call a round table of these and other senior people and try for a consensus. A consensus would in turn enable IIMC to launch a full time course in Advanced Journalism and even to start a full fledged department. It would be the first such venture in India, and indeed the world, a truly pioneering effort. Here is a gist of some of the responses received.

1. **Prem Bhatia:** Very comprehensive... "in fact I recall having mentioned this subject to the Director at the last convocation. I am happy... ."

2. **M.V. Kamath:** "It is an excellent idea. ...should include the following apart from what is mentioned in the syllabus: (a) learning of an additional language, (b) exchange of experiences."
3. **S. Nihal Singh:** "Knowledge of the effect and impact of computerisation should be an important part, apart from what has been provided."
4. **Pritish Nandy:** "Advanced Journalism is a different trade from subediting and reporting and requires methodical training."
5. **Vindo Mehta:** "Visualisation is all important. ...your course will be unique."
6. **Kamlendra Kanwar:** "Objective of Advanced Journalism input is very sound, should be more work related."
7. **K.N. Radhakrishnan:** "Exposure to the more successful among practitoiners of Advanced Journalism is very necessary."
8. **Khushwant Singh:** Too busy to write but willing to make a contribution at any round table that the IIMC organises."

Before the round table stage was reached, however, the Dhenkanal decision was taken. Inevitably I went to the new place and plunged into the 16-hours-a-day seven-days-a-week task of starting a new campus and making it stand on its feet. With this the Advanced Journalism course and department had to be put on the backburner, where it remains, since the date of my superannuation intervened and Dr Yadava, after serving three four-year terms as Director, went back to his department as Professor of Communication Research. I am still willing—both the spirit and flesh are still strong – to take forward the project of the Advanced Journalism course and department, but it is for others to decide.

Dr Yadava is only the second man above 50 in age I have met in my working life who has a young brain in his head. The other was the late Durga Das, who retired as Editor of the *Hindustan Times* and founded the feature agency *India News and Feature Alliance* (*INFA*).

Here is how I discovered the greatness of Durga Das. A friend named Vijai N Shankar and I had in 1967-68 devised a model named *Prosatoon,* or a pocket cartoon in prose. We thought it was a marvellous idea like the Page 1 pocket cartoon, which had been thought of by D.R. Mankekar when he was sent to the struggling Delhi edition of the *Times of India* in 1950 as its Editor. Mankekar had motivated cartoonist T. Samuel to draw for page 1 the original pocket cartoons which are now such a fixture in all major dailies.

Shankar and I perfected our *Prosatoon* by writing one topical piece everyday and then presented the prototype to Mr Kuldip Nayar, who was then the *Statesman's* Resident Editor in Delhi. Alas, he did not think highly of it.

Shankar lost hope and gave up the attempt but I trudged on. Finally I approached Durga Das. He thought highly of it but wanted to make sure I could write one piece a day. "Mail me one piece everyday," he said when I met him. "I will look critically not only at the piece's quality but also at the post office stamp on the letter to make sure you are churning out one piece a day."

Durga Das the legend

I accepted the challenge and for the next 20 days posted him one piece per day. On the 21st the mail brought a post card asking me to meet Durga Das.

He told me he was convinced I could produce one good *Prosatoon* piece a day but some of the editors to whom he sent *INFA*'s features might not be equally innovation-minded, "Why not write a longer light piece every week? We will include it in our weekly envelope. When it is established we can move on to the daily piece."

From Prosatoon to Birbaliana

I agreed. It took me three months to work out the format and the theme. Those were days when Dr Christian Barnard of South Africa had carried out the first ever successful heart transplant. If a heart could be transplanted from one body to another, why could man not be transplanted in time?

I transplanted Birbal, one of Emperor Akbar's *Navaratnas*, from the 16th century to the 20th and made him match his wits with it.

After writing several pieces to reassure myself I could do it, I waited for Durga Das to finish the book on Sardar Patel's correspondence which he was then editing. I was keen to present to him my prototype so that "Birbal transplant" could get going. Even as I waited, the morning papers reported one day thar Durga Das had died. A man past 70 with the agile and innovative brain of a 25-year-old !

Birbal Transplanted

The Birbal transplant series saw the light of day, but not through *INFA*. Durga Das had been succeeded by his son Inder Jit who, could not appreciate what the brilliant old man saw in the series. The weekly series was ultimately carried for many years by the *National Herald*, then edited by Hari Jaisingh.

I rank Dr Yadava with good old Durga Das in this respect. His contribution is that he appreciated the need for training journalism students in devising whole Communication Packages. Up to that time, and even now in places where old-style journalism teachers are entrenched, training in the basics of reporting and what is called "subbing" (subediting) is all that is provided. In institutions where the need for training in devising Communication Packages is provided, the students come out knowing that innovation is the spice of journalism.

Another advantage of training in Advanced Journalism is that the trainee learns to divine what the audience needs, something that many in the audience themselves don't know. As *Outlook* Editor Vinod Mehta says, if the reader knows what he wants, why is he reading this magazine? He would go to Encyclopaedia Britannica and read the relevant portion. Or he would log on to the Internet.

And now to some case studies to show how Advanced Journalism works.

SON RISES TO THE OCCASION

"Father was young spirited, vigorous and dynamic until his end. He left people half his age panting for breath by his pace—and ideas.

"(He) did edit Sardar Patel's Correspondence. ... in ten volumes. But he was keeping indifferent health.

"In fact, he was disinclined to take on the job. But he agreed when Morarjibhai and Maniben Patel, Sardar's daughter, called on him at his residence, and pleaded that he alone could do justice to the job.

"Durga Dasji finally agreed and told them: 'Now you should pray that the Almighty should give me a long enough life to complete the task.' God granted him his wish."

INDER JIT, *INFA* Editor
and son of Durga Das

CHAPTER VI
Captaincy Counts

After the disastrous tour of New Zealand by Azharuddin's Indian cricket team, Manager Bishen Singh Bedi remarked that the whole team should jump into the Pacific Ocean. When Azharuddin took another team to England everyone wondered what made him put England to bat in the first Test after winning the toss. It was generally agreed by commentators that this mistake of the Indian captain shaped the course of the Test series resulting in a humiliating defeat.

Yet Azharuddin is one of the most talented of batsmen and an electrifying fielder. He obviously has proved himself to be far less talented as a captain.

Every jawan who is a great fighter need not become a great general, every outstanding cricketer need not be a good captain and every good subeditor or reporter need not be a great Editor.

I cite Azhar's example because I expect those who read this book to be more familiar with cricket than with many other things. Dilip Vengsarkar was another five-star batsman who made a zero-star captain. Kapil Dev on the other hand, has proved to be both a good cricketer and a good captain.

Father of 'bodyline'

Cricket is full of such contradictions. Douglas Jardine was a cricketer who could barely make it to England's Test team. Yet when sent to Australia in 1933 as captain he devised the "bodyline theory" to which the star-studded Australian team including the immortal Bradman had no answer.

England has produced many such examples. Norman Yardley was a mediocre cricketer who could barely make it to England's Test team. Yet he succeeded the great Walter Hammond as his country's captain. Other such England captains in post-war cricket have been Ray

Illingworth and Brian Close. Yet an immensely gifted cricketer like Ian Botham was made captain and then had to be dethroned.

India likewise has had good cricketers like Bishen Singh Bedi and Mansur Ali Khan Pataudi who made good captains, good cricketers like S. Venkataraghavan who made bad captains, and ordinary cricketers like G.S. Ramchand who as captain outfoxed even the wily Richie Benaud. There were, then, Sunil Gavaskar and, much before him, Vinoo Mankad who, weighed down by the responsibility of saving the side for long stretches of their careers, made too-cautious captains.

I can recall strikingly similar cases in journalism. I had been an avid reader of the weekly *People* in 1955 and 1956. It had a distinguished pedigree. Founded by Lala Lajpat Rai in 1929, it had had well-known names as its Editor—Lala Feroz Chand and Rana Jung Bahadur Singh and finally the legendary K. Rama Rao.

Even Rama Rao, who was a great journalist and a greater Editor, could not make it come anywhere near R. K. Karanjia's *Blitz* and D.F. Karaka's *Current,* which in the 1950s ruled the Indian world of weekly newsmagazines. When the *People's* proprietors could bear the financial burden no longer, Rama Rao left with most of his team. Gian Singh became Acting Editor with a leaner team. Even he could not sustain it. Finally he also left. Anser Kidwai, a young man, took up the reins as Acting Editor.

I admired the freshness which Kidwai imparted to the *People.* Once I visited Lucknow, where the *People* was published, in 1956. I complimented Kidwai on his effort but suggested some improvements. I realise now it must have sounded jarring to him coming from a journalist who had only been a freelancer and had had no experience of production. But with his delicate Lucknow culture in which being rude, or even uncomplimentary, is just not the done thing, he was courtesy and politeness to a fault.

Salary: Two Meals a Day

Within months of this the *People* ceased publication. Kidwai moved to Delhi to work for another periodical. This happened, I think, in September or October 1956. In early January 1957 I was passing through Lucknow and went to the *People's* office. The Managing Director, Niranjan Lal Gautam, was very frank. He said there was no money to pay the editorial staff, therefore there was no magazine. The press, a hand-setting outfit, was however there.

I offered to work without salary. To the great glory of Niranjan Lal Gautam, he said he would not want anyone to work free of cost. He said he could give me two meals a day.

And so I set out reviving the weekly. Working from 6 in the morning to 12 midnight, I managed to write enough of political and economic stories, book and film reviews, sports and business articles to keep pace with the composing.

On the fourth day the foreman, Kanhaiya Lal, came to me for guidance on make-up.

Did I have to guide the make-up too? I had no idea how it was done. In fact I had never been inside a printing press. Kanhaiya Lal reassured me. The problem, he said, was that the press had lead type for only five or six pages at the most. Unless the pages were made up and printed and the type distributed, no further composing was possible.

This was my first lesson in production. I learnt the mechanics of it from Kanhaiya Lal. I also learnt reporting and selling space because I was one of only three men on the job—proprietor Niranjan Lal Gautam, part-time accountant Shuklaji and myself.

I slept in the office, unfolding the holdall every night about 11 and folding it up at 5 next morning. After a quick wash, I would be ready for work at 7 a.m. No tea, no breakfast. About 1 p.m. I would go to the restaurant where my two meals were to be given to me. After lunch I would go out reporting, returning about 6 p.m. to proofread the composed matter and prepare copy for the next day. It would not be before 10 p.m. that I would have the second of the day's meals which had been promised to me.

From Editor to Deliveryman

Copies of the magazine would be ready printed on Friday afternoon. Now the third of the three jobs I was doing began. Piling up copies of the magazine at the back of the office bicycle, I would pedal away from bookshop to bookshop, collect payments for last week's sales, pick up any unsold copies and give copies of the current issue.

The shopkeepers were skeptical to begin with. The *People* had not been coming for four months. For at least six months before that it had either been coming late or skipping issues. The regular readers had drifted away. So had the advertisers.

I employed the technique of not disclosing that I was the new Editor even while I was the deliveryman. "A bright new Editor has come," I would say, citing the more important of the news stories I had written in that particular issue. "Give him a try. In any case you have nothing to lose. I will take back any unsold copies next Friday, no questions asked."

It worked. Sales rose steadily rather than spectacularly. But I noticed with great relief that they never went down. Shops which began by taking four copies were, at the end of six months, selling 15 to 20 copies a week. The readers slowly drifted back. So did the advertisers.

Working as a one-man editorial department, helping the proprietor obtain advertisements and being the lone man in the circulation department helped me get an insight into the working of a newspaper or magazine organisation. I learnt that—

A. Unique among consumer products, the cost of production of a newspaper/magazine is higher than the sale price. The loss is made up by advertisement revenue.
B. Deadline is a unique feature of a media organ. If the *People* was ready after the deadline, as happened once, its value plummeted to zero. The shopkeepers on that occasion were not only annoyed but angry.
C. A cake of soap has to conform to the standard set. That is, each cake of Lux must be exactly like another cake of Lux. But one edition of the *People* had to be different in content and form from any other edition (though the format and masthead remained the same). That is, one edition of the *People* must look like another edition, yet the content and make-up had to be new every week.
D. Unlike consumer products, the *People* influenced public opinion. It was a thrill to hear people discuss in coffee houses, restaurants and buses things I had written about them and others in the *People*. I was still unknown in the city as the Editor of the *People*. In any case I was so absurdly young—only 22—that no one suspected I was doing that job.

The five major departments in the *People* were interdependent, yet they had to function independently to fulfil the common purpose. These five were: (a) the news department or editorial, (b) the advertisement department, (c) the circulation department, (d) the press, and (e) accounts. The first and third were manned by me alone and in the advertisement department I helped out.

I discovered that .each of the five involved specialisation. The technique I used to get news or views were very different from the techniques I needed, for instance, to obtain advertisements or to persuade shopkeepers to sell more copies.

Yet there had to be a joint strategy to perform the following functions:

A. Jointly identifying the audience to be serviced (in this case the Lucknow readers, advertisers and booksellers).
B. Jointly servicing the same audience.
C. Maintaining a healthy teeth-to-tail ratio. (in the *People,* we were all teeth with no tail thanks to the shoestring budget).
D. Ensuring the availability on time and at all times of all the necessary inputs so that the deadlines could be met without sacrificing quality.
E. Ensuring the avoidance of waste (there was hardly any waste because we were perpetually short of funds).

In the next 30 years, my conviction grew that captaincy counts as much in a daily or weekly as in cricket. Indeed a team—in cricket, in war or in a newspaper—is only as good as the captaincy, other things remaining the same.

Vijay Hazare, who is one of the legends of Indian cricket, recalls in his second book *A Long Innings* the case of Nawab Iftikhar Ali Khan of Pataudi (father of Mansur Ali Khan Pataudi who later also became India captain).

The Nawab of Pataudi was most unexpectedly made captain of the Indian team to tour England in 1946. "Pataudi, with all his past standing, was not an active cricketer in India," recalls hazare. "He proved to be the best skipper off the field by the sparkling wit, (his) standing as a prince and as an ex-England cricketer who had obtained a Test century on debut against Australia."

Hazare, with his natural humility, does not say explicitly how good the Nawab was on the field as captain. But one can glean this from the instances cited in the book about the Nawab's doings on the field. A little before going to England as the captain of the 1946 team Pataudi had declared, as North Zone skipper, the innings closed at 300, though this was not allowed if the rules were applied strictly. He was himself batting at the time but he "retired" voluntarily. Hazare's comment: "I have already said in the early part of this chapter that such a thing is not done in big cricket."

Captain's Whim

During the England tour, Pataudi did many thing as captain which Hazare cites. In a match against Surrey, "without any prior intimation and trial, the captain asked me to open the innings with Merchant... Although I had faced the new ball quite effectively on many occasions, I had by then usually settled down. Normally I batted at the No. 4 position, and it is a cricketing axiom that the batsmen normally do not want their position in the batting order changed unless forced to do so... The experiment was a failure. I was promptly disposed of before opening my account."

Hazare cites the instance of the Second Test at Old Trafford, Manchester, where the Nawab won the toss and "took the unusual step of sending the opponents in!" England made 236 for 4 but next day were all out for 294.

Merchant and Mushtaq Ali gave India a rousing start. But then "Pataudi had another brain wave and decided to alter the batting order radically. He promoted Kardar (the babe of the team) to No. 3... It did not quite come off and Kardar failed, to be followed by the rest of us...". In India's second innings Pataudi did the hat-trick of the unfortunate decisions made by him in the Test and came in No. 3... Both he and... opener Mushtaq Ali fell with the total at 5".

Now look at what home team skipper Walter Hammond did. Vijay Merchant was India's ace batsman and in great form. He was adept at wearing down the bowlers and then grinding them to the dust. Hammond watched him in county matches and studied his strong and weak points. Weak points he did not seem to have many, so Hammond decided to make a chink in his armour out of one of his strong points!

England had lost all its pace bowlers during the six years of World War II though most of the Test batsmen remained—Hammond himself, Len Hutton, Denis Compton (who served in India during the war and played for Holkar) and Joe Hardstaff. The spin bowlers were also lost, so England depended upon ageing D.V.P. Wright. Good old Paul Gibb, though not too efficient, was full of ideas behind the wicket.

Doing duty for England with the new ball were the ageing Dick Pollard, the Lancashire fast bowler, and the new boy Alec Bedser of Surrey. Bedser was a very accurate fast-medium bowler who could bowl to specifications.

Hammond had studied Merchant very closely. In his big repertoire of strokes, Merchant had the rare leg glance which he executed to perfection. Those were days when no one had thought of the helmet for fielders at vulnerable positions, so shortlegs were rarely employed. If the fielding captain did employ a short leg, the batsman concerned would become wary.

Hammond's Masterstroke

Hammond took bowler Bedser and wicket-keeper Gibb into confidence. Bedser was to bowl a good length ball coming in on the leg stump. Such a ball could not be pulled or hooked and it would be risky to drive it. Yet it was the ideal ball for a leg glance.

Before bowling such a ball, Bedser was to give a signal to wicket-keeper Gibb, who would move stealthily as the ball was being bowled to where shortsleg would be. Having briefed Bedser and Gibb, Hammond moved to his familiar position at first slip.

Bedser went back to the start of his run up, turned, gave the pre-arranged signal and bowled. As he delivered the ball, Gibb moved left to position himself at short leg. As planned, it was a good length ball moving in. Merchant saw it as the ideal delivery to make a leg glance off. He did so with relish, thinking of the four he could get, or at least two runs if the fine leg fielder could cut it off.

Merchant was a batsman who believed in keeping the ball on the ground. He rarely, if ever, hit a six and was caught only if he misread a ball or miscued the shot. There was no occasion when a Merchant shot was executed to go up in the air.

The leg glance was, however, another matter. There were no short legs to contend with, so the leg glance could be on the carpet or uppish to begin with, later on racing towards the boundary along the carpet. This particular leg glance was also a few feet above the ground. It found its resting place in the waiting gloves of Paul Gibb.

The back of India's batting was broken. For, despite the presence of talented batsmen in Lala Amarnath, Vijay Hazare, Mushtaq Ali and

Vinoo Mankad, India depended heavily on Merchant's stabilising innings.

Merchant seemed dazed as he looked back at Gibb waving his glubbed hands triumphantly clutching the ball. It was not until the third Test that Merchant got over the jinx caused by this dismissal and scored a century. And this happened, let us remember, to a batsman who was the highest run-getter in that wet England season, scoring seven centuries, the largest number by anyone that year, and logging more than 2,000 runs—which was higher than the runs scored by Hammond, Compton, Hutton, Hardstaff or Washbrook, the leading batsmen in England then.

In 1948 the Indian cricket team went to Australia. This time the captain was Lala Amarnath. Australia's captain was the redoubtable Don Bradman, great as skipper and greater as a batsman.

The Indian team encountered Bradman in only the second match of the tour. This was at Adelaide against South Australia whose captain Bradman was.

"Here we made a mental note of the way Bradman studied the opposing batsmen," Hazare comments. "After I had despatched a couple of short ones to the midwicket fence I saw a perplexed look on Bradman's face." The captain's mind was obviously at work to figure out how to get Hazare out.

Bradman the captain had not exercised his mind in vain. Came the first Test at Brisbane. Australia had made 382 for 8 when Bradman declared. The reason was that a "tropical downpour and the subsequent drying up process had turned the Gabba wicket into the typical 'sticky dog' or 'the gluepot' as is the Australian term for it."

Bradman's strategy worked. Ernie Toshak, a left-handed medium pacer, did the Indian Test team in, capturing five wickets in the first innings and six in the second. Hazare's comment: "Without detracting from Toshak's merit it is only fair to state that he himself was a novice to such conditions and in the previous Test against England on the same ground Bradman actually took him to the wicket and asked him to bowl at a particular spot!" The success was Toshak's, the tactic was the captain's.

The second Test at Sydney was to prove a battle of wits between two brainy captains. After India had scored 188 in the first innings, Australia were caught on a rain-affected sticky wicket and were all out for 107.

"The wicket was still bad," observes Hazare, "Amarnath adopted the unorthodox policy of opening with the tail-enders".

The idea was to let the sticky wicket take a toll of the tail-enders. After it dried out the top order batsmen could come and score enough runs. At 61 for 7, India still had a lead of 140 runs. But then it rained some more, turning the wicket sticky again.

"Bradman looked happier with every shower," observes Hazare. And no wonder. The rest of the match was washed out and Bradman's Australia escaped batting on a sticky wicket which could have caused a collapse.

Hazare does not mention it but Arthus Mailey, the former Australian Test cricketer and commentator, remarked that Amarnath had outfoxed Bradman in captaincy and had had Australia in a spot. Had the last stage of the match not been washed out Australia could have found it difficult to wriggle out of the trap laid for them by Amarnath.

The battle of wits continued in the next Test at Melbourne. Australia scored 300 in the first innings and India began with a first wicket partnership of 124. Then, Hazare says, Bradman had a "brain wave". Defending a small total, he put Barnes on to bowl to Hazare.

Bradman's 'Barnes Trick'

"Now Barnes was not a regular bowler and not certainly a Test class one at that," writes Hazare. "His memories of bowling could not have been pleasant because the only time he was seriously called upon to bowl in a Test he saw England setting up an all time record of 903 at the Oval before the 1939 war".

But bowlıng skill is one thing and captaincy skill is another. Bradman who, as mentioned earlier, seemed puzzled when Hazare had sent two short-pitched balls to the midwicket fence in the match against South Australia, may have worked out a plan to get him out through Barnes.

Barnes bowled a "near googly", as Hazare records. "I hooked out and was caught". Skipper Amarnath came in next. "Surviving onc ball he was beaten by another freak delivery and was plumb lbw."

This is what a captain can do. Study the weaknesses of a batsman or bowler and work on it.

It is not my purpose to say that captaincy or editorship consists only of such strokes of genius. If one is a genius, he is bound to click in any case. The point is that captaincy or editorship is a discipline all by itself. It can be learnt, mostly by studying the work of those who have been successful in this trade.

'Brick by Brick'

To be sure, every good captain or editor has had his waterloo. Kuldip Nayar, whose *Grievances* column proved to be the work of a genius, also introduced in the *Statesman* a column called *Brick by Brick.* The idea was brilliant. It was to show the reader that despite all the bad news of accidents, frauds, political chicanery, etc., which made it to Page 1, there were good things being done to build up the country.

It was a contributory column. Reporters and Special Correspondents were supposed to provide short—one or two sentences—items on something worth while which had been done to build up society. Subeditors were expected to write out pieces for *Brick by Brick* from news agency reports, from the reports of outstation, foreign and other correspondents and from the reports of stringers, (which means part-time correspondents.)

Ultimately, and inevitably, the baby fell into the lap of the Chief Subeditor. You can't have a column containing only one or two such pieces. So he had to rig up two or three more. The big problem was that the concept was not clear enough to most reporters or subeditors. It had not been spelled out.

As in all cases, it was left to the Chief Subs to identify news items or parts of them which could make the *Brick by Brick* column, and then to get them rewritten for the purpose. Some items contributed by reporters would be rejected or rewritten, some were rigged up from agency or stringer copy.

An additional problem was that no credit line was given for contributing to the column, though there was a payment of five rupees per item used. It was a small payment, but not as small as it looks today. This was in the sixties when journalists' salaries ranged from Rs. 500 to Rs. 2,000.

However, it is not money but motivation which makes the mare go, and the motivation was lacking despite the money. Night after night the Chief Sub, faced with the fact that people working through the day were able to find only one or two items for the column, had to rummage through the copy to find any news which could qualify to be a "brick".

Frequently he had to settle for items which he would otherwise not use at all.

This was one reason why the column remained anaemic. But probably the vital reason was a defect in the concept. Anything which showed the nation being built brick by brick deserved a bigger write-up than a paragraph. In that paragraph one could tell in brief what happened but not answer the questions "why', "how" and "who". Neither those who created the column nor those who read it were satisfied. In fact I suspect that most readers who read it cursed the paper for telling them only part of the story.

Kuldip Nayar accepted defeat. Instead of blaming reporters and subeditors for not implementing one of his projects, one day he agreed to discontinue the column. He had achieved success with his *Grievances* column and with the many exclusive stories he gave to the paper, either himself or by tipping off his reporters. With *Brick by Brick* he gracefully accepted the basic flaw in the concept and let it die. Both, to my mind, are hallmarks of a great Editor.

MENTIONED IN DESPATCHES

Editorship consists not merely of humouring people. The *New-Bedford* (Miss) *Standard Times* publishes the name, address and photograph of every Bedford area resident who is apprehended on a drug felony rap. It began in 1991. By January 1993 some 2,300 Bedford residents had thus been mentioned in despatches.

CASE STUDIES

CHAPTER VII

MID-DAY Sunshine

The Sun rises at dawn. *MID-DAY* rises at noon. Right ?

Right, but inaccurate. *MID-DAY* is designed to be a lunch time addiction, so it hits the Mumbai streets between 12 noon and 1 p.m.

James Augustus Hicky, founder of the *Bengal Gazette,* India's first newspaper, couldn't have dreamed in 1780 that a lakh of adult Mumbaikars would one day be pining to get a copy of *MID-DAY* to go with their lunch everyday. Indeed, he couldn't have dreamed even of the breakfast time addiction of millions all over India to their morning daily.

The *Bengal Gazette,* to quote Dr S.N. Ghosh,* first Indian Editor of the 130-year-old *Pioneer*, was a weekly lampooning sheet "causing considerable annoyance to many and great commotion and excitement" in the small community of British traders, military men and administrators then in Bengal.

Lord Macaulay described Hicky and his tribe as catering to a "public opinion" which meant the "opinion of of 500 persons who have no interest, feeling or taste in common with the 50 million among whom they live ...." James Stewart Mill told a House of Lords committee in 1832: "The English newspaper press in India is the organ only of the English society ......It has little to do with the natives and the great interest of India."

The sprouting, in the wake of the *Bengal Gazette,* of the Indian language press made many people newspaper-conscious, though sparsely. Then Macaulay's famous formula spread the English language in India. With it came English dailies. These dailies and the Indian language dailies reporting things of interest to Indian readers made for the newspaper reading habit.

*In the chapter *The Press, Then And Now,* in *Communication-2000 A..D.,* edited by the author.

The addiction came with World War II. The world was at last changing on a daily basis. With the army, navy and air force expanding manifold, prices scaling unheard of heights, scarcity of most commodities of mass consumption, and Germany and Japan advancing rapidly towards India, everyone wanted to know everyday what was happening, and what was likely to come.

Khalid A.H. Ansari, who was publishing the Urdu daily *Inquilab* in Mumbai, reasoned that if a morning daily could become a breakfast time addiction of people, there was scope for a daily lunch time addiction.

Come to think of it, addiction to a daily newspaper was a revolutionary idea. Emperor Aurangzeb and Shivaji, and all their predecessors and successors for many generations, had never read a newspaper. Indeed there was no newspaper in their time.

Revolutionary Idea

If addiction to a morninger was a revolutionary idea, a lunch time addiction was doubly revolutionary. But Khalid Ansari had revolution in his genes. His father Abdul Hamid Ansari had been a freedom-fighter who had, on Gandhiji's Quit India call, published in his *Inquilab* the recipe for making the bomb! His contention was that India must be freed, without the bomb if possible and with it if necessary.

The revolution in Khalid Ansari's genes had surfaced even before he had created *MID-DAY*. I remember that in 1964 when I came to Delhi *Sport and Pastime,* the weekly sports magazine published by the *Hindu* from Madras (now Chennai), was still being published. Cyril Flory, the sports editor of the *Statesman* in Delhi, was its senior sports correspondent in Delhi. Henry Daniell and K.N. Mohlajee were the junior correspondents. But the weekly was on its last legs. The theory was propounded that India did not have a fertile soil for periodicals, specially niche magazines. *Sport and Pastime* closed down.

Khalid Ansari cocked a snook at this theory. It was the vision and the Communication Package that mattered, not the soil. He launched *Sportsweek,* a weekly which specialised in personalised and behind-the-scenes reporting of sports. *Sport and Pastime* had mostly carried a round-up of the week's sporting activities. Sports-loving readers naturally abandoned it.

Khalid Ansari's *Sportsweek* was such a roaring success that other sports magazines sprouted, one of them published by those who had closed down *Sport and Pastime* only a few years earlier. Buoyed by *Sportsweek's* success, Khalid Ansari dreamed of a lunch time daily. What would it contain that the morning papers did not have?

The morning papers carry the most important of the news which breaks out up to 2 a.m. the previous night. Until at least 5 hours after 2 a.m., India generates hardly any news because it is sleeping. Only the Americas generate news after 2 a.m. Indian Standard Time because it is day time in the New World. But only some of this news is of interest to Indian readers. For *MID-DAY* the useful news from the New World has to be received, edited, composed and put in the pages by 9-30 a.m. After 9-30 a.m. there is time only for printing and distribution if the paper is to be in the hands of the reader by lunch time.

A second channel of fresh news for *MID-DAY* could be night time road and rail accidents and crime. The third channel could be exclusive stories.

After Khalid Ansari and his dedicated team had made a success of the paper in Mumbai, an edition was launched in Delhi in March 1986. I headed the Delhi editorial team.

I discovered that the first hurdle was the unreadiness of the news agencies, PTI and UNI, to feed a daily which was locked up at 9-30 a.m. Since Delhi, and in fact no city in India other than Mumbai, had a lunch time daily, the news agencies sat over the overnight copy. Only a junior subeditor would come at 8 a.m. or so to keep a general watch. The full editorial shift would come only at 10 a.m. and start selecting, editing and feeding news to subscribers.

Work with UNI

I went to Kalkur, the then Chief Editor and General Manager of UNI, and volunteered to come and feed to subscribers by teleprinter the news which was likely to be of use to a lunch time daily. In time I and the UNI subeditors whom Kalkur put on duty from 7 a.m. managed to creed by 9 a.m. 8 to 12 news items of use to a lunch time paper.

The next step was to alert the Delhi police, railway and roadways officials to be available and well briefed early so that our reporters could get overnight news from them in time. This was not easy to organise since almost all senior officers would be in the bathroom or at breakfast at 7 to 8 a.m. Even on moving to the place of work, they would take time to be briefed on overnight happenings. Newspapers had to be briefed or handouts had to be sent only about 5 p.m. since all dailies were morningers.

MID-DAY reporters and I told them we wanted all the overnight reports, specially crime, latest by 9 a.m. Many of the police officers were reluctant to accommodate *MID-DAY*, for who wants to start working at 7 a.m.? They did not relent even when I told them that I reached *MID-DAY* office bang at 6.55 a.m. everyday without fail. It was only when we told them that if they could not give us the overnight crime news by 8-30 a.m., or latest by 9 a.m., we would have to depend on sources in the many *thanas*.

This scared the police officers, since the *thana* briefing was bound to be incomplete and lop-sided and would not give the complete picture. Worst of all, it could give the police a bad name.

I cited a factual example. There had been two dacoities in Wazirpur between 10 p.m. and 2 a.m. one night and the affected people had telephoned me at *MID-DAY* at 7 next morning. When the reporter concerned contacted the DCP, he didn't know anything about it. Even the Station House Officer of the concerned *thana* said he didn't know about the dacoities. Would he want *MID-DAY* to report that four hours after the dacoities both the DCP and the SHO were unaware of them?

That did it. The DCPs and ACPs, even the Police Commissioner, agreed to move out of bed early to be briefed about overnight crime before *MID-DAY* telephoned.

About exclusive news stories, we perfected the strategy to obtain them, just as the Mumbai editors and reporters must have perfected their strategy many years earlier.

Two-fold Strategy

Our strategy was two-fold. First, visualise what the morningers would not plan to do about a news event. Most morningers are content to report what they are briefed with or see. We decided to go beyond the briefing and the sighting. When General A.S. Vaidya was killed in Pune two pro-Khalistan activists were arrested for it. The morningers duly reported it and promptly forgot about the event until the court hearings began. We decided to report exactly which specific crime they were to be charged with plus the details of the police version. One day passed, two passed but the reporter concerned, the Chief Reporter and I decided not to give up the quest. On the fifth day the reporter came back with the whole charge-sheet hurriedly copied from the supposedly confidential document.

Then, one summer, there was a shortage of water in Delhi which was much worse than normal. All the morningers carried general reports of the shortage, and as usual water supply authorities issued general denials. Chitra Gopalakrishnan was covering it for *MID-DAY*. She and I devised a plan to be more specific in our reporting. She would ring up friends and acquaintances in various localities every morning to find out specific details. Then we would telephone water supply authorities telling them of specific details including the names of our informants, the house numbers and the exact hours and minutes when there was no water supply. This was much more difficult to deny and only general denials came. A typical report filed by Chitra ran as follows:

"Though the water supply authorities issued the expected general denial of water shortage in Delhi, *MID-DAY's* inquiries show that water supply in Greater Kailash, Janakpuri and West Patel Nagar was restricted to one hour from 7 a.m. to 8 a.m. in the past 24 hours as testified to by Mr X, Ms Y and Ms Z....."

Zail Singh's Clarification

The next part of the strategy was to follow up the major news stories published by the morning papers. One morning all the morningers quoted Giani Zail Singh, who had by then demitted office, as saying that at one stage during his feud with Prime Minister Rajiv Gandhi, Rs.40 crores had been collected for use in toppling him.

I telephoned Gianiji first thing in the morning since I knew he was an early riser. He said he had told reporters Rs 40 crores had been on offer or could have been collected for the purpose. When I told him I was ready to send a reporter to gather more details, he fixed up a time in the afternoon. But that would be too late for *MID-DAY*. What he could do was to tell me the details, and I would write out the story and send a copy to him for authentication.

I did so and sent reporter Ajay Jha with the copy to Gianiji. Meanwhile the story was composed and corrected and we waited for Ajay's phone call giving the go-ahead. The call came at 9-15 a.m., saying Gianiji wanted only two minor changes. The changes were made and the story was splashed on Page 1. Thus, within a few hours of reading the report of the Rs 40 crore collection, *MID-DAY* told readers of the full details and the finer points, complete with names.

One other thing which we did to create exclusivity was a column named *Citizen Extraordinary.* I would interview selected persons, whether celebrities or others, who had done extraordinary things. The first piece in the column had the headline *Boy Who Refused To Cry.* It was about a school child who had been crushed by a bus which severed one of his legs. That boy, I discovered, had refused to cry or be disheartened throughout the treatment, including the fitment of an artificial leg. He is, incidentally, now in America and doing well for himself with his artificial leg.

There were pieces in this series about celebrities like Kapil Dev (*How To Become A Superstar)* and Giani Zail Singh (*Story Of A Mason's Son).* There were also people who had done extraordinary things but who themselves were not celebrities. Among them were Sitesh Alok and Aruna Sitesh, a couple who were publishing a non-profit magazine containing translations in English from current literature in various Indian languages. Still another piece was about a *Barefoot Engineer,* the story of the struggle of Prem Chand Srivastava, a senior engineer now, who had only one set of clothes during school days and no shoes, and his wife Vineeta.

The U.S.P.

MID-DAY's USP (Unique Selling Proposition) consists of the following:

A. *MID-DAY*'s lunch time addiction which is unique in India except for a contemporary named *Afternoon Despatch and Courier,* started by *Busybee* Behram Contractor, which followed its success and is giving it good competition in Mumbai.
B. The further developments in the news stories reported by the morningers. This gives readers the feeling of being updated up to the minute.
C. The packaging of what is essentially a magazine as a daily.

The first two, as discussed, give the reader the sensation of change. The last-named, namely a magazine packaged as a daily, is a clever device not tried before with any success.

In the morning only two pages of the day's edition are made up, the first and the last. These contain the very latest news which usually takes off where the morningers left off. It is smart to keep the first page and the last for the morning, for they constitute the packaging.

The rest of the daily consists of magazine-style writing and pictures The pages constituting the magazine part are written, composed and made up the previous day, and the positives are kept ready. As soon as the two pages reserved for the morning are put together, their positives are also prepared. The positives of all the pages, that is those prepared in the morning and those prepared a day earlier, are then plated and printing starts.

The typical *MID-DAY* editorial day starts at 7 or 8 a.m. and the concentration is on the first and last pages. As soon as they are ready, the day's edition is out of the way of the editorial department, which from 10 a.m. onwards focuses its attention on the inside pages of the next day's edition.

CONCENTRATION OF FORCES

All successful military campaigns are based on concentration of forces. Mao Zedong's peasant army was outnumbered by Marshal Chiang Kai-shek's army which additionally had the latest U.S.—supplied weapons. But Mao's hordes concentrated on one Chiang stronghold after the other and made the defenders flee. Hitler's blitzkrieg consisted essentially of overwhelming the enemy with vastly superior armoured troops, superior both in numbers and arms. Napoleon won all the battles he won by concentrating his forces. At Waterloo Marshal Nye tarried in following instructions. Napoleon consequently was not able to achieve concentration of forces and paid the price.

No wonder Mao's favourite saying was: "If all the Chinese exhale together there will be a storm."

MID-DAY concentrates all its energy up to 9.30 a.m. on the two pages reserved for the morning hours. From 10 a.m. it concentrates all its forces on preparing the inside pages for the next day's edition.

CHAPTER VIII

HT Sheds 'The' Fig Leaf

On February 21, 2001, the paper which readers had known as the *Hindustan Times* for 76 years shed the 'The' to become plain *Hindustan Times*. The type faces also changed, the masthead type change being the most pronounced. An explanatory note by the Editor, carried on the front page itself , explained why. It said the paper's credo was "change with continuity". The attempt in making the change which gave the paper a new look was to make it look "neater, smarter and more contemporary".

OUR NEW DESIGN

At the Hindustan Times, our credo is: change with continuity. It is in that spirit that the HT unveils its new design today. We have tried to make the paper look neater, smarter and more contemporary without resorting to gimmickry or visual stunts. Our intention has been to preserve the essentially serious and sober character of the HT while making the news easier to read.

When the decision to redesign the paper was taken last year, we were determined to hire one of the best newspaper designers in the world. Our search ended in Washington DC where we engaged Michael Keegan, the highly regarded head of design and Assistant Managing Editor of one of the world's finest newspapers, the *Washington Post*.

Michael made two long trips to Delhi and spent several months working with the HT's editors and artists to evolve a design that seemed international and contemporary while simultaneously preserving the HT's traditional character as the market leader: as the paper people respect and trust.

The new body copy typeface is Nimrod, a popular choice around the world though no other paper in Delhi uses it. The choice of headline typefaces was slightly more complicated. Michael selected Miller and Knockout. Both these were unfamiliar to Indian newspaper editors and were not even available in the country. Not only did the HT have to import the typeface, one version of Miller was specially commissioned and designed for us.

We imagine that it may take readers a little while to get used to the new design. But we are sure that you will find that North India's best-selling paper now not only looks much smarter, but that the news has become much easier to access.

Happy reading!

Vir Sanghvi
Editor

What else does the change consist of ? There are fewer shoulders, which is welcome. Every Editor in every newspaper discourages shoulders, because it is basically laziness which makes subeditors fall back upon shoulders. The few shoulders that are there have as many as four lines under them, which amounts to underlining a word or expression four times. This should logically have resulted in making it shoddy, but surprisingly that is not the effect. The HT Editor argues that the redesigning is the work of an expert brought from Washington. Point conceded. Examples are:

HT EXCLUSIVE and **LIBERHANS TESTIMONY**

The body type face chosen is Nimrod which makes the text look cleaner than what it was in the earlier *avatar*. The imported headline type faces make the headlines stand out without being ornate. Specially the italics version of the headline type is far superior to the earlier italics version which looked ornamental.

For some reason the old style of carrying the dateline and byline of briefs at the bottom, right flush, has been retained. The only change is that the byline and dateline have gone italics from the bold earlier. In the process one or the other of the four Ws (who, where, when and why) and one H (how) tends to get dropped.

It is no one's case that these questions should be answered in the intro itself, as editors used to insist earlier. The norm now is that the answers to these questions should be available to the reader somewhere in the top half of the news story. But since the briefs consist of only the intro, these answers should be woven in the intro itself. That is why a full dateline (not merely the name of the place) and the byline are more necessary in briefs than in longer news stories. Consider the following briefs incorporated in the February 21 issue itself:

Glenn wants it short

AUSSIE bowling spearhead Glenn McGrath said he would like to bowl in five-over spells at a time in Test matches during the Indian tour so that he can conserve enough energy in the prevailing humid conditions. "At this jucture of my career I would not want to bowl long spells and it is very tough for a fast bowler to bowl long spells in humid conditions on batsmen friendly pitches," he said.

PTI, Mumbai

When? Where?

A second example of this blemish creeping in in the briefs is:

Delhi are champs

DELHI WON the 46th national school cricket tournament under-14 for boys by defeating Chandigarh by three wickets. Chandigarh were bowled out for for 98 in 32.1 overs. Gurkirat (21) and Simrat Bawa (17) were the main scorers. Delhi bowlers Vartik Tihara and Ashutosh claimed two wickets each. Delhi reached their target in 31.5 overs with Prem (31) and Kartikeya (23) did the bulk of the scoring

PTI, Vijayawada

This is an unnecessary sacrifice of meticulousness which HT has opted to continue to make despite "our new design".

One tends to overlook such aberrations when change is not being contemplated, but when change is worked for, and when experts are entrusted the job, it is more

THEN

THE HINDUSTAN TIMES

FEBRUARY 2001 METRO www.hindustantimes.com Also Published from Patna and Lucknow

S CAT ORDER IRECTOR

WORLD

'TALIBAN AGREES TO HAND OVER OSAMA TO S. ARABIA' P15

KAPIL R PLAY CHA

President ou

NOW

Wednesday, February 21, 2001

Hindustan Times

Rs 1.50 NEW DELHI METRO

World, p13

CLINTON'S WOES GO...END FOR

than ordinarily necessary to correct inaccuracies and plug the loopholes which make inaccuracies possible.

But the major flow in such a change is that it tends to remain cosmetic, and therefore ephemeral unless accompanied by a change in content. It is like renaming Connaught Place and Connaught Circus after Indira and Rajiv Gandhi. What difference has the change made? People tend to forget cosmetic changes as fact as they notice them because without a change in substance things remain what they were.

When I was Editor of the *Pioneer,* the Chief News Editor would frequently make a cosmetic change or two whenever I was away. The radio programme was headlined *Radio*. He changed it to *Aerial* once I was away. Then he changed the headline of the TV programme to *Antenna.*

The pitfall in such changes is that the man who does them derives great satisfaction from the excerise thinking he has revamped the paper, whereas readers care little for such changes. Once in my absence the Chief News Editor changed the byline of the Chief Reporter to *By our Staff Correspondent* while retaining the reporters' byline as *By a Staff Reporter.* When I returned to headquarters I was informed of this, whereupon I asked each visitor to my office for two days running whether he/she was happy with the change. Not one of the visitors—and it was normal for me to get about two dozen visitors in a 15-hour working day—had so much as noticed the change. There was no question of being happy or unhappy.

When a layman becomes a journalist he notices, or is told, that all English language dailies take the definite article before their name and that the definite article is capitalised in the case of *The Times* (of London) and of no other paper. The reason is that each daily is part of a crowd of similar newspapers from which the reader chooses one. The only exception was Edatata Narayanan of *Patriot*, which calculatedly dropped the definite article, and later Mumbai's *MID-DAY*. *Patriot* was the only one of its kind—remember the standard make-up, the standard four-column lead headline, the selection and display of news which were different from other papers', and the exclusive Communication Package. Similarly *MID-DAY* was the only one of its kind when started. One may or may not agree with what Narayanan did in *Patriot* or what Khalid Ansari did in *MID-DAY,* but the reasoning is clear and logical. Now the *Hindustan Times* has dropped the "The" and changed the typefaces without a change in the content. The contents remain substantially the same. Consider the following:

Depleting tribe of true politicians

POLITICIANS ADEPT in the art and science of government have become a rarity here. Most of them indulge in short-term gains to amass wealth.

A lower-rung politician here, hooked in a rape case, got Congres ticket for the Assembly election. However, he lost the election.

The only qualification of the said politician was wealth earned through real estate business. He also happened to be the younger brother of a former MLA.

A big leaseholder of Silica mines here, became a Minister in the State for six months without contesting poll.

Then, he managed a Congress ticket and became an MP. His brother, facing court cases, joined INLD and won Assembly election and is now a Cabinet Minister in the State.

Haryana is a sort of trendsetter in politics. Almost all the CMs groomed their wards in politics as extra constitutional authorities. Later, they were promoted as MLAs, MPs and Ministers. The crop of politicians of the stature of Gandhi, Bose, Dr Prasad is no longer to be found.

HTC, Faridabad

Is this news or comment? Or a plant to vilify some politician? And consider the following:

Son throws out parents from their own house

Neeta Sharma
New Delhi, March 16

BLOOD TIES can be snapped in a second for lucre. Ask 75-year-old Raghunandan Prasad Aggarwal, a heart patient, and his 73 year-old wife, a diabetic, they will tell you all about it.

The old man, along with his wife, was thrown out of his house which he had built from his hard-earned money. The culprits were his son and daughter-in-law, who wanted to acquire the property.

The drama was enacted before the Delhi High Court last week when the division bench took a serious note of the matter and directed the police to throw the illegal occupants (son and daughter-in-law) out of the house.

"What is happening to our society? It seems that children these days do not take care of their old parents," observed a division bench of Justice Usha Mehra and Justice M A Khan.

According to the writ, the old couple has not only been restrained from entering their own house in Shalimar Bagh but were also physically assaulted by his son Navneet Kumar and his daughter-in-law.

The writ filed by Aggarwal further alleges that he and his wife were threatened by their own son and their daughter-in-law as they did not change their will.

But what is even more agonizing for the old couple is that despite having three sons they have no place to go.

"We have been discarded by all of them so we went to Hardwar and are presently staying with our daughter," Aggarwal has stated in his petition, adding that when they reported the matter to the police they also did not help them. So they approached the Delhi High Court.

In the last date of hearing, the court had issued notices to the state had asked Delhi Police to file in their reply.

The Delhi Police also expressed its helplessness and said that when they went to Aggarwal's house Navneet informed them that it was a family matter.

Additional Standing Counsel (Criminal) Mukta Gupta informed the court while defending Delhi Police's stand on the matter.

The bench, while dictating the order, also expressed surprise over the fact that the son and the daughter-in-law of the old couple have not only misbehaved with them but also were not permitting them to enter the premises, despite the fact that the property in question was the property acquired by the petitioner himself.

"Under the circumstances, directions are given to the police to give full protection to the petitioner by removing the unauthorised occupants from the house of the petitioner, be that his son or daughter-in-law," the bench stated.

Is this news or an oldtimer's sad commentary on the bad ways of the world? Both have found a place in the post-remodelling. *HT.*

LAW OF TANTALISATION

I waded through 4 months' supply of four dailies and a number of periodicals for 4 hours to get the Feb. 21 copy of HT. I got the Feb. 19 and 20 issues and thought I was zeroing in. Then the Feb. 22, 23 and 24 issues. I lost hope and mechanically thumbed the half a dozen issues left. Lo and behold, there was the Feb. 21 issue. Law of Tantalisation!

The law says if you are waiting for a bus on route 720, you will get 721, 722, 719 but not 720. When you are about to lose hope 720 will come—but running in the opposite direction. Only when you have lost all hope will the 720 come, Law of Tantalisation again!

CHAPTER IX

Military Matters and Wordless Cartoons

One of the less known achievements of General J.N. Chaudhuri who retired as Chief of the Army Staff in 1966, is a process of educating lay people in military matters that he undertook for 14 long years. From 1951, when he was commanding an armoured division in the rank of major-general, to about November 1961, he wrote a series of articles in the *Statesman* telling the layman how to assess and evaluate military matters. He became Army Chief following the 1962 debacle against China.

In 1965, while still Army Chief, he wrote three more articles for the same paper, but for a different reason. Throughout—from 1951 onwards—he wrote under the byline "By Our Military Correspondent". Only two persons apart from the General himself knew who the Military Correspondent was—Alfred Evan Charlton who had made the arrangement in 1951, and the Editor of the paper. It was not until the General himself chose to disclose the fact that the world came to know who the *Statesman's* Military Correspondent was.

Charlton had been a middle-level Editor in the *Statesman* in 1951. A few years later he became the paper's Resident Editor in Delhi and then he brought off another editorial coup in collaboration with Philip Crossland, his News Editor.

Fateful Encounter

It was customary for All India Radio in invite distinguished journalists including foreigners to make broadcasts in its External Services meant for listeners in other countries. Crossland made one such broadcast. As he came out of the recording room, a tall young man presented him a sketch of his face hurriedly done as he sat recording his broadcast. Crossland looked at the sketch, then at the young man, then again at the sketch, and remarked: "You made me look almost handsome." The young man made appropriate noises protesting it was a faithful sketch of his face.

Then Crossland asked the question which changed the young man's life: "What do you do"?

"I'm an announcer", the youth said in his measured, cultivated voice.

"You are wasting your time. Come to the *Statesman*".

This was in 1956-57. The young man had had dreams ever since he had been a student at Allahabad University in 1952-54 of being a famous radio broadcaster, perhaps another Melville de Mello. He had the right credentials. He had a very good broadcasting voice which he had further cultivated carefully. Though a day scholar, he had got himself attached to the famous Muir (now Dr. Amaranatha Jha) Hostel while at the university. Thus he was a member of the exclusive, much-envied "ex-Muirian" club. But the world was such that nobody had spotted his obvious class and he was still an announcer.

Situational Humour

He went to the *Statesman* in response to Crossland's invitation. The big man explained the project. He was to draw pocket cartoons which depended for their humour on the situation alone. Anyone could be funny with words. He should be special. He should not use any word either inside the cartoon or as a footnote. The subject should be non-political and relate to the life of the common people. There were to be five such cartoons every week, to be published together every Wednesday on the local page as a feature. The name of the feature was "*Out of my mind by Sudhir Dar.*"

Sudhir Dar, for that was the name of the young man, drew the cartoons religiously for many weeks. He was paid well too. But somehow he was not fully satisfied. He went to Bombay as a Sales Executive with Air-India. Here also he was not satisfied and returned to Delhi and back to freelance cartooning.

For one year or so, "*Out of my mind*" continued to be a weekly cartoon feature on Page 3, the local page. Then, one day Charlton, who was Resident Editor, asked him, "Are you now ready to move on to Page 1?" Sudhir was.

On January 1, 1962, the *Statesman's* Delhi edition looked different. On Page 1, at the bottom of column 1, there was a mischievous cartoon under the headline "*Out of my mind by Sudhir Dar.*" From that day onwards, one cartoon in the series was published each day on Page 1. No written word was allowed. Sudhir squeezed his brain dry trying to wring humour out of it for his cartoons. Most days it was a hit.

Historic Letter

One day a letter landed on the Editor's desk. It read—

To the Editor , The Statesman
New Delhi
Sir,
Who is out of his mind? You
or Sudhir Dar?
Yours faithfully....

The letter was published in the "Letters to the Editor" column and created what ultimately turned out to be an avalanche. The first letter on "*Out of my mind*" was followed by a trickle of other letters, some funny, others pontifical, trying to interpret the unique cartoon feature or see meanings in individual cartoons. The trickle became a stream, then a flood.

The Letters to the Editor column just couldn't handle the flood. As one bunch of letters was published, another landed.

One day Sudhir was given a bunch of letters and asked to draw wordless cartoons incorporating the more funny of the ideas of the letters. Then, one morning, the *Stateman* covered the whole of the local page with those letters laced with Sudhir's illustrations. It is unlikely that there has been any paper in the world which has devoted the whole of the local page one day to "letters to the editor" on a single topic. It must be the first and only one in the history of journalism.

But enough was enough. At the bottom of this historic page went a two-line note saying, "Regretfully, this correspondence is now closed—Editor".

The series went on from 1962 to 1967. When Charlton became Editor-in-Chief (they call it only Editor in old fashioned *Stateman* style), *Out of my mind* began getting published in Calcutta also. A typical cartoon of the series showed a bus being driven in pouring rain. In place of the windshield wiper there was a cow sitting on the roof vigorously wagging its tail, thereby wiping the windshield of the water!

The achievement of Crossland and Charlton was to give to their readers a series of daily pocket cartoons the like of which were not seen before and have not been seen since. They harnessed the genre of wordless non-political cartoons of evergreen situational humour for a specific purpose. This is Advanced Journalism at its most brilliant.

To be fair, it was D.R. Mankekar who had first thought of a daily Page 1 pocket cartoon. This was when he was Editor of the Delhi edition of the *Times of India* in 1950 and commissioned cartoonist Samuel to produce a pocket cartoon a day for Page 1. Before that, the big political cartoon, carried almost daily, had been made part of the Communication Package of newspapers by the legendary Shankar. But the daily non-political pocket cartoon was Mankekar's idea.

The innovation and advance for which Crossland and Charlton must get credit is the further refinement of the idea to get a wordless pocket cartoon a day of situational humour for daily newspapers. Nowadays no major daily in any language thinks itself to be complete without the non-political pocket cartoon. The men who thought of it at first were Mankekar and, in the case of wordless cartoons, Crossland and Charlton.

To revert to Charlton's other achievement as a practitioner of Advanced Journalism, General Chaudhuri has compiled 45 of the articles he wrote for the *Statesman* as its Military Correspondent between 1951 and 1961, plus two which he wrote in 1965, in his book *Arms, Aims and Objects*. In the introduction, he explains how he came to write them.

How it Happened

In 1951 he was commanding an armoured division on the border in Punjab during one of the "periodical low ebbs" in Indo-Pakistan relations. One day, while in Delhi on a routine visit, he dropped in at a cocktail party at the house of the British head of Burmah-Shell named Sinclair.

"Sinclair introduced me to Evan Charlton of the *Statesman*", General Chaudhuri writes, "and after a bit Charlton asked me if I could suggest the name of someone who would write a fairly regular column for them on military affairs. The articles were to be non-political, easily understandable, to leave Pakistan alone and to arouse an interest in military matters. Charlton felt this was necessary in a newly independent country where, in the past for political reasons, the intelligent citizen had for generations been kept out of anything concerning defence. We talked it over and finally I offered to do them myself. Both Charlton and Sinclair swore I wouldn't be able to cope with the work but this made me all the more determined to see if I could."

Further, General Chaudhuri writes: "My anonymity was very well kept. Even on the *Statesman,* apart from the Editor and one other, no one knew who was writing these articles."

When General Chaudhuri was appointed Army Chief rather suddenly on November 10, 1962, following the debacle against China, "my career as a Military Correspondent had to come to an end."

An Army Chief

As Army Chief he made certain suggestions for the protection of the country's borders in peacetime, principally the creation of para-military forces to take care of occasional instrusions, smuggling, etc., and to keep a general watch. Then Pakistan intruded into Kutch in force in early 1965, and to keep up action on his suggestions for policing the border, he wrote an article in the *Statesman* as its Military Correspondent in April 1965. The subject was "An Integrated Police Force for Border Defence".

"I have no knowledge as to whether my strategy was effective", the General writes, "but things did start to move faster!"

By early July 1965 the main decisions had been taken and "the follow-up was for the officials, including myself, to work out the details. To give this process a helping hand, I wrote the next article. The headline of this second article was 'Policing and Military Duties of Border Force'."

Appropriately, the second article, published on July 8, 1965, begins as follows: "The remark about a prophet being without honour in his own country applies with even more force to a mere newspaper correspondent. However, from time to time a thought put forward is taken up or else the law regarding coincidences is getting too close for comfort."

The *Statesman's* Military Correspondent, Gen. Chaudhuri, further writes: "Readers of this column may remember a suggestion regarding a border police force that was argued out on April 22. It is pleasant to find that State Home Ministers recently agreed to the raising of such a force. It is hoped that some of the other suggestions made at the time regarding organization might help the backroom boys now putting the scheme together. The object of today's article is to discuss some questions of training, equipment, and, finally, the biggest aspect of the whole problem, command and control."

Editor's Contribution

There are two purposes behind relating these incidents illuminating the style of working of Charlton. First, it shows what a tremendous contribution the practitioner of Advanced Journalism can make to enriching the paper when he visualises the needs of his readership and proceeds to make arrangements for their fulfilment. Secondly, it is pertinent to note that rather than spending his time writing frequent editorials or signed articles which many others like Assistant Editors can do, the Editor makes a far bigger contribution by concentrating on enriching the Communication Package.

I had joined the *Statesman* during the fag end of Charlton's editorship. The talk among the subeditors and reporters, some of them disgruntled, was that the man was an "illiterate" Editor. The reason was that he had written perhaps only two or three editorials during the two years he had been Editor and probably no signed article at all.

One obvious reason, of course, was that he was an Englishman whose feelings and perceptions might not be in tune with the thinking of his Indian readers. But the major reason, to my way of thinking, was that he followed the principle of division of labour. He concentrated on doing that which no one else on the paper's staff was qualified or authorised to do, leaving to the latter that which both he and his Assistant Editors could do. Students of economics know that this is the best way to maximise satisfaction from the efforts of any team of workers. The theory of division of labour says so, and all trade, including foreign trade, is based on it.

CHAPTER X

The UNI Story

Kuldip Nayar, now a best-selling author of books on political developments and a columnist who is published in many countries, had been an information officer in the Government of India for 10 years until 1964. In his last posting he was attached to Lal Bahadur Shastri, then Home Minister of the Government of India (Shastri later became Prime Minister). Nayar had spent his time well, making friends, influencing people, observing things and making notes.

He left Government service in 1964 to head the fledgling news agency United News of India as Chief Editor and General Manager. In fact, one of the Directors of UNI had told him it was fated to close down after failing to find its feet in the first three years (1961-64). The reason given was that PTI, the other and bigger Indian news agency, was too well entrenched for UNI to make a breakthrough.

Before Kuldip Nayar, UNI had been headed by D.P. Wagle, a veteran of PTI who had for long periods been the agency's UN correspondent before retiring. A venerable figure, he was steeped in PTI culture and could not think of ways of working to create an image of UNI which was different.

Key Question

Despite the grim warning, Kuldip Nayar joined UNI. He asked himself the key question which every Editor everywhere must constantly ponder: "Why should anyone—newspaper, radio or other subscriber—take UNI service?"

Obviously UNI, with its far fewer correspondents and scarier resources, could not beat PTI at its own game. It had to play a game in which it could outgun and outdistance PTI.

Kuldip Nayar studied PTI closely. The agency gave long reports on most news events it reported. Its coverage of the national scene particularly was far more comprehensive than UNI's. If a newspaper could afford to subscribe to only one news agency, it had to be PTI. Even for those who did not have the constraint of resources, it would be a waste to subscribe to a second news agency giving substantially the same news package.

Kuldip Nayar drew up three rules of thumb for UNI reporters, subeditors and News Editors.

First, no UNI story should normally run to more than two "takes" unless it was the text of some important resolution or speech. In rare cases a story could run to three "takes", but no more.

Sounds innocuous? The first implication is that the UNI reporter would try to condense every news story he has into 400 words or so which means more concise and crisp writing.

It would also mean each reporter would finish writing his story earlier than he would if he were free to file four, five or six "takes". Other things remaining the same, the UNI story would tend as a rule to be earlier on the teleprinter than the same story done by a PTI reporter.

A corollary to this is that if all or almost all news stories of UNI are, say, 25 per cent shorter, UNI would as a rule be able to creed all, or most, of its stories earlier than PTI.

Anyone who has produced a newspaper knows that the Chief Subeditor, harried by the approaching deadline, tends to use that version of a news story which lands first—unless the version which comes later has substantial new points, in which case the earlier version sent for composing is supplemented by additional news points taken from the later story. In only rare cases does the Chief Subeditor/News Editor scrap the earlier copy and send out a new story based on the later version.

Space Constraint

A factor which made the impact of this decision snowball is the space constraint in newspapers. Other things remaining the same, any subeditor in any newspaper would want to use the shorter version of a news story instead of racking his brain trying to cut and prune the longer version to the desired length.

The result of this one innocuous-looking decision was that the UNI credit line became progressively more common. Sometimes a newspaper would use the UNI story and at the tail of it add a few paragraphs saying "PTI adds". What is more, those newspapers which did not subscribe to UNI started wondering whether it would not be better to subscribe to this news agency also.

The *second* rule of thumb which Kuldip Nayar prescribed was that UNI should try to give at least one exclusive news item at the national level per day, even if it was minor, and one exclusive news item from one of the state capitals. With his extensive contacts in the Government, he took the lead. Apart from his duties as Chief Editor and General Manager, he worked as a reporter in the evenings and would return to office at nine, 10 or later in the evening to file exclusive news stories.

One such story concerned the division of East Punjab into Punjab and Haryana. The commission seized of the problem had recommended such a division. Kuldip Nayar got to know of it and filed the story late one night. As expected, attempts were made next day by bureaucrats and politicians to deny the story, but UNI was on firm ground. All that it had done was to say that a division had been recommended; it did not say that the Government had decided to make such a division.

This and other such stories created a sensation and many a newspaper started wondering whether it was not being penny wise not to subscribe to UNI's service.

Exclusives from States

The exclusive from the state capitals also started coming. Since there were 16 to 17 states at the time, it meant each bureau in a state capital had to look for just one exclusive story in two weeks if UNI was to give its subscribers one exclusive state-level news story a day.

The *third* rule of thumb was for every reporter to help the News Editor on duty compile a "Budget" of news stories to be expected along with approximate wordage. Every morning UNI would creed to subscribers the "Budget" of the stories to expect, the time they were likely to mature and the approximate wordage.

In the evening a "Revised Budget" would be creeded listing the additions to the morning "Budget" and the deletion of particular stories which did not or were not likely to mature. This was again a great help to newspapers in planning their editions.

Apart from these rules of thumb, there were other decisions which had a far-reaching impact. UNI could not match PTI or the bigger newspapers in pay and perks to its journalists. He calculated that, to keep morale high, the least it could do was to give personal bylines liberally whenever a reporter did an exclusive, or even an out of the way, story. It was designed to provide motivation and a sense of participation, and he says it did both these jobs. Nayar's UNI was thus the first Indian news agency to give personal bylines to reporters who did good work. When some paper somewhere in the country used the personal byline, the reporter concerned felt compensated for his comparatively low pay and perks.

Newsy Image

I remember that whenever in charge of an edition in a daily, I would defy conventional wisdom to carry the UNI personal bylines on a selective basis. What for? Because, as everyone should know but most people do not realise, an edition is as "newsy" as its image. If the reader thinks it is "newsy", it *is* "newsy" whatever the pundits say. And personal bylines play a big role in creating an image of newsiness.

Two other decisions are worth mentioning. PTI had a tie-up for foreign news with Reuter, the British news agency, and UNI with AP, the American. PTI had a few foreign correspondents and UNI none at all. Hence UNI's foreign news coverage tended to be an unabashed dishing out of much of what AP gave.

Kuldip Nayar decided UNI could have a few stringers (or part-time correspondents) abroad even if it could not afford a full-fledged fleet of staff or Special Correspondents. It would, he calculated, tend to give a degree of exclusivity to UNI's foreign news coverage as compared to PTI, and it did.

He also issued instructions to the desk to cut out propagandist or slanted words, passages or paragraphs from AP's news stories. In the long run it tended to add credibility to UNI's foreign news coverage.

Another innovation was to start the day by creeding to UNI subscribers the message, "Good morning, subscribers; India's population today is...". This was calculated on the basis of the average growth rate per day.

Those who are thrilled today by the Doordarshan Morning Show's population clock should realise that UNI did this a quarter century ago.

It was meant as a social service, says Kuldip Nayar, to make Indian media professionals conscious of the population problem. Today it is fashionable to cry oneself hoarse about the galloping population. A quarter century ago, when talking of the population problem was not in fashion, it required some imagination to start the day like this.

It must have done its bit to arouse consciousness of the problem, for, to Kuldip Nayar's surprise, some newspapers started using the day's population figures in their news columns as creeded by UNI!

K.P.K. Kutty, who is General Manager and Chief Editor of UNI now (1993), talks of those days with nostalgia. He was a subeditor in Indian News Service (later Express News Service) when UNI was founded in 1961. He migrated to the new news agency as a reporter.

UNI in the beginning was able to afford teleprinter circuits only from Delhi to the bureaux in the state capitals. Once a story landed at the UNI office in the state capital, it was replicated and a messenger would go round the city by bicycle to deliver copies to various newspapers. Even in Delhi, reporters were asked to make several copies of their reports. One was, of course, edited and creeded to various centres (Lucknow, Chandigarh, etc.) as justified. The others were given to a messenger who would then pedal away furiously to the offices of the *Hindustan Times* and the *Statesman* (the only two subscribers in Delhi) to deliver copies. And if the messenger was not there, Kutty or another reporter would go and deliver the copies.

Kutty says it was the coming of Kuldip Nayar as General Manager and Chief Editor which made the difference. Newspapers which were subscribing only to the PTI service increasingly started feeling they were missing things by not subscribing to UNI. Those which subscribed to both and had earlier found little difference between the two now gave up any idea of discontinuing UNI service. For UNI had become different—and therefore valuable.

Drift Checked

Kuldip Nayar's stewardship checked the drift of the news agency towards oblivion. It also meant consolidation. The danger of disintegration was over, for solid foundations had been laid. The news agency had now more offices in more towns. But what kind of offices? Kuldip Nayar elaborates: "Many UNI bureaux were run by a person who acted as manager, correspondent, (teleprinter) operator and even messenger."

Kuldip Nayar asked the six newspapers which had sponsored UNI for more money for investment. This they did not provide. What they did to help out was to release their subscriptions in advance when the news agency was in financial trouble, which was most of the time. Salaries were disbursed in instalments.

Kuldip Nayar's innovation made UNI take root, but it was still a fragile plant.

In 1967 Kuldip Nayar got an offer from the *Statesman* to become its Resident Editor in Delhi. The money was three times as much as UNI was giving him. Kuldip Nayar told the UNI proprietors he would stay on if they gave the news agency more money for expansion and diversification. He offered to give a written undertaking to this effect.

There was no response from the Board of Directors. Instead, the Board authorised S. Mulgaoker, one of the Directors, to offer to raise Kuldip Nayar's emoluments to the level he was being offered by the *Statesman*. Nayar's response, as set out in the Silver Jubilee (1961-81) commemorative volume of the news agency, was: "I refused to accept the raise. How could I when I had driven the employees like slaves and could not offer more than a pittance of a salary to any? I left UNI in 1967."

Exit Nayar, Enter Mirchandani

Kuldip Nayar's departure meant the end of a pulsating era. It also marked the beginning of an equally dynamic, though different, era. His successor was G.G. Mirchandani, who had been like Kuldip Nayar a Government servant though for a longer period.

At UNI Nayar had worked as a reporter also. Mirchandani did not, but he had consummate managerial skill. "Give me a good news agency, I know how to sell", was the *mantra* he chanted before subeditors and reporters. He was methodical, dedicated, hard working and enterprising. He also had vision and instinctively knew what would be valued by subscribers.

Once, as an Assistant Editor of a daily I visited Mt Abu, Headquarters of the Brahmakumari organisation, to find out what this outfit was up to. The provocation was a thick rumour that it was a front organisation for a group which was indulging in extra-legal activities. The occasion was one of the world conferences that the Brahmakumaris periodically held. The year was 1983, and the place was swarming with members of the organisation as well as outsiders, both Indian and foreign.

I was surprised to find Mirchandani there, and not only was he there, his news agency was represented by reporters and a temporary teleprinter connection which churned out a dozen stories a day based on the activities of the 3,000 delegates who met in open session and in workshops and discussion groups on specific subjects. PTI was unrepresented, so UNI had a dozen exclusive stories, human interest and other, each day for a small expense.

Mirchandani not only exhorted his journalists to work hard, he ensured that they did. UNI reporters thereupon coined the following rhyme:

One story a day keeps Mirchandani away
Two stories a day keep Mirchandani gay
Three stories a day earn you more pay.

Apart from the stories filed by reporters, there were something called the "Dollar Stories." These stories were filed by deskmen who were promised Rs. 7.50 by way of conveyance for each story of theirs used, whether they spent any money on conveyance or not. They were called "Dollar Stories" because the American dollar those days fetched Rs. 7.50!

This gave the desk plenty of stories to choose from, enriching the UNI Communication Package. What is more, subeditors' stories invariably tended to be off-beat—those which PTI and newspaper reporters usually did not cover. This strengthened UNI's exclusivity which Kuldip Nayar had tried to establish with considerable success.

'Chasing Diary'

One of the trump cards of Mirchandani—and this is a lesson in Advanced Journalism—was a "Chasing Diary" which he maintained. In it was entered every task he entrusted to anyone or expected anyone to do. Everyday the entries would be reviewed, and an entry would be struck off only when the task was done. If a reporter was entrusted a task one afternoon, and by the end of the next day it had not been done, Mirchandani would look at the "Chasing Diary" and ask the reporter concerned what had happened.

This simple device ensured that any idea coming from anyone which Mirchandani asked a reporter to chase was never forgotten. Far too many Editors and News Editors in far too many newspapers let many ideas die because they do not maintain a "Chasing Diary".

Two things should be obvious to everyone from this but may not come to mind immediately. First, if a man produces an idea which the Editor accepts as chaseable but which is not chased, the man would become cynical. And not only he but everyone else. For, it means the Editor is not all that serious when he says "yes" to an idea. The result will be that the stream of ideas would slowly dry up. Those who have ideas would keep them to themselves, and many who could produce ideas would think there was no point in squeezing one's brain if the idea was to remain an idea.

Many newspapers and other media organs live by reflex action, repeating the routine day after day, and in the process producing fossilised editions which are no advance on what they did a week ago, a month ago or a year ago. That is why, the *Telegraph* succeeded with ridiculous ease in rolling back the *Statesman* empire in Calcutta when it pursued new ideas and implemented them. That is why UNI has become so big a rival to PTI within as little as a quarter of a century.

If Idea Not Chased

Another result if an idea if not chased is that the Communication Package provided by a news agency becomes predictable. It loses it excitement and freshness. This is the complete opposite of what it should be. For newness is the life and soul of a news package. Anyone running a news agency should be constantly looking for new things to report.

Even as Mirchandani was expanding UNI's network came the Emergency. To keep tighter control over news, Mrs. Gandhi merged UNI, PTI and two other news agencies into one conglomerate called Samachar. UNI's head office was closed and its workers were instructed to report to PTI. All UNI bureaux in towns and cities around the country were locked up, and later surrendered to the landlords. So when the Janata Government came to power in 1977 and undid the merger, UNI had to start all over again—without any offices anywhere except for the head office in Rafi Marg which was reallotted to it. Yet such was the impact of the news agency made under Nayar and Mirchandani that within a fortnight of its reopening it got back 268 of its 500 pre-merger subscribers.

Mirchandani, while out in the cold following UNI's merger with PTI to form Samachar, had started a backgrounder service called *India Backgrounders*. When UNI was revived and Mirchandani returned to head it, he converted this rather successful backgrounder service into UNI Backgrounders. In 1981 he started Univarta, a Hindi news agency owned by UNI. Next he wrote to Doordarshan offering to make newsclips for its News and Current Affairs programmes, a project which fructified several years later under Kutty.

It was also during Mirchandani's regime that the coverage of Pakistan was substantially strengthened. The device was to install powerful radio receivers to monitor Radio Pakistan transmissions from both the western and eastern (now Bangladesh) wings.

It proved to be invaluable during 1971 when the Pakistan army cracked down on Dacca intellectuals and politicians. On the day of the crackdown Radio Pakistan kept studiously silent on developments in Dacca but gave one clue. At the end of one news bulletin late at night, it said Admiral Ahsan (a Bengal officer) was no longer Governor of East Pakistan. UNI latched on to it and issued a news item saying, "Admiral Ahsan, the Bengali Governor of East Pakistan, has been removed from his post..." It was a world scoop.

UNI's Secret Source

This and other such items of Pakistan news based on radio monitoring made UNI's New Delhi-datelined Pakistan news acceptable and credible to the world. Kutty says now that it was buttressed by a secret source in Dacca. His name, which UNI kept secret for two decades until Kutty told me in 1993, was Moosa, then News Editor of a Dacca daily. UNI would just make a late night trunk call to Moosa, who would tell it of the day's happenings in Dacca, something which Radio Pakistan blacked out. The Pakistanis were foxed how UNI could find out about Dacca happenings despite the iron censorship enforced by the Pakistan army.

Mirchandani was succeeded as Chief Editor and General Manager of UNI by U.R. Kalkur, a newsman to his fingertips but not a great administrator. The silver lining was that Kalkur was aware of this shortcoming, so he entrusted the administrative chores to his next in command, Kutty.

Kutty pursued the initiatives made earlier with vigour. The UNI photo service, in association with AFP, began on September 9, 1987, 23 days ahead of the PTI photo service.

When Kalkur died in 1989 Kutty became chief executive and went on with great energy to expand, diversify and modernise his news agency. A scan service and a graphics service were started. Computerisation of the news agency was taken up with vigour.

But perhaps the biggest thrust in Advanced Journalism was made by UNI's decision to go in for foreign operations. It decided to enrol subscribers in West Asia and elsewhere. Starting with mailers, it has slowly established a foothold in Dubai, Kuwait, Bahrein and Qatar. It is now a full-fledged news service beamed to its foreign subscribers via satellite. This made UNI the first Indian news agency to have regular subscribers abroad—the first stage of a national Indian news agency going international, thanks to Kutty.

The result of these initiatives is evident from the revenue generation, which was Rs. 6.8 crore in 1988-89 and is expected to be double this figure in 1993-94.

We know of UNI today as a thriving news agency competing on equal terms with the much older PTI. All those who brought UNI to such a relatively comfortable situation made a contribution. But if the Editor is the first among equals, he must make more of a contribution. Kuldip Nayar, Mirchandani, Kalkur and Kutty certainly have made king-size contribution.

COME ASIANS, BE AMERICANS

The Quincy (Mass) *Patriot Ledger* has for four years been teaching Asian immigrants, who are pretty numerous in the area, how to be good Americans. To begin with they must learn English, so the paper carries English lessons for newcomers and tips on how to pass American citizenship examinations.

The bonus: Asian immigrants become *Patriot Ledger* readers even before they know English properly, and much before they become American citizens.

CHAPTER XI

'I've a Grievance, Sir'

From UNI, Kuldip Nayar moved to the *Statesman,* Delhi, as Resident Editor. I had joined a few years earlier and had started taking charge of editions.

To us juniors, it seemed a mystery why a man who was Editor and General Manager of an established news agency should want to be the Resident Editor of a daily. Nayar told me recently why. He had worked for the Government and knew what it was like. He had now worked for a news agency and mastered the art and craft of it. He now wanted to master the print medium.

Among the first things he did was to have a survey made of readers of the *Statesman*. Those days the *Statesman,* particularly the Delhi edition, was considered the best edited paper in India. Teachers told their students to read the *Statesman* to improve their English. People who competed for entry to the civil services read the *Statesman.* It was compulsory reading for civil servants, diplomats, military officers, politicians and for all decision-makers in both the private and public sectors. Bengalis read it because it was believed that nothing could happen in Bengal without the *Statesman* learning of it, whether it published the news or not.

'Consult the *Stateman*'

But the biggest tribute to the *Statesman* of those days was paid by peer journalists working for other papers or news agencies. The unwritten rule in every newsroom in Delhi was "when in doubt, consult the *Statesman*". It was the final arbiter in all disputes concerning the usage of words or phrases and regarding the construction of sentences. If the *Statesman* used it, it was English. Similarly about spellings. If there was a dispute whether the spelling was Khrushchev or Khrushchov, the commonest way to end it was to pick up the *Statesman* and see which spelling it used.

Reporters and subeditors of the *Statesman* were looked up to by their peers as perhaps a superior breed. When a vacancy occurred in the *Statesman,* virtually all subeditors and reporters in Delhi applied. When I joined the *Statesman* in 1964, I was the 35th person tested for one vacancy.

But, for all these impressive claims, the *Statesman's* Delhi edition sold only about 45,000* copies per day (Calcutta's figure towered in lakhs). The *Hindustan Times* sold more than one lakh copies. The *Times of India* and the *Indian Express* were distant silver and bronze medallists, sometimes interchanging their medals. The *Statesman* came fourth. Kuldip Nayar wanted to know why. Another mystery was the persistence with which the figure of 45,000* stuck to the *Statesman.* Whether we missed stories or scored over others, the circulation did not change.

Once there was an industrial dispute and a lock-out in the Delhi *Statesman.* It lasted three months. Most of us feared that we would lose readers by the thousand. Perhaps we would be left with only 10,000 to 15,000.

The day the lock-out was lifted, the print order was a hesitant 30,000* copies. In the next few days demand kept rising. By the end of the week circulation was back to 45,000.*

Reader Survey

The reader survey ordered by Kuldip Nayar solved both these mysteries. Many readers said they kept the dictionary by their side when they read the *Statesman.* This meant two things. First, the English-speaking elite who cared for the nuances of the language bought the *Statesman.* Second, the paper was bought by those who sought status through being seen reading it, even if they read other papers in the closet.

The third category of *Statesman* readers were those whose news figured frequently in its columns—armed forces officers, Bengalis, senior bureaucrats, politicians, diplomats and the traditional aristocracy. Apart from these, no one went anywhere near the paper. In fact many readers were inhibited entering the forbidding red building at the confluence of Barakhamba Road with Connaught Place's Outer Circle.**

*These figures are only an approximation and not officially verified, since circulation figures are considered confidential.

**This building has since been demolished and in its place there is now a multi-storeyed structure.

The obvious remedy, if we wanted circulation to rise, was to use simpler English. Kuldip Nayar issued the necessary instructions.

Most oldtimers in the *Statesman* were outraged. We did use simple idiomatic English, didn't we? Isn't it Queen's English to say "Wolf in sheep's clothing" or "ask for one's pound of flesh"?

Sometimes some of us punned in the headlines. Achyut Menon (alas, he is no more) once gave the headline "Black sheep in wool trade", meaning that there were only some traders in wool who indulged in unethical practices; the rest were honest.

One of my headlines which clicked was "Honours won and lost on walk-overs; Delhi hockey affairs get curiouser and curiouser". I was using an expression made famous by Churchill.

Charlie Banerjee gave a cricket headline "Sita Ram causes State Bank crash". G. George wrote out the headline "Grand old graduate" over a news item which said a man had graduated at the age of 60.

When General Suharto ordered all hippie-style hairdo in Bandung lopped off, a joint effort by Bannerjee and myself produced the headline "Bandung mops up the mop".

Yash Paul Narula, who became News Editor in 1991 but migrated to the *Hindu,* was at one time a subeditor in my shift. He edited the story of the Jimmy Carter-Edward Kennedy tussle for Democratic nomination for the U.S. Presidency and gave the headline "Carter sure of party ticket, Kennedy surer." The first part referred to the virtual majority Carter had got, the second to Kennedy's claim he was still sure he would make it.

Indlish or English?

When Kuldip Nayar issued instructions to use simpler English, some of us started asking whether it meant going back to prosaicism. Would we have to say, "Bandung hippies' heads being shaved"? Or "Carter gets majority but Kennedy claims the can still win"?

Some of the diehard oldtimers angrily commented that this man, unsteeped in the *Statesman* tradition, wanted the paper to be published in *Indlish* instead of English. Others said if we followed the instruction—they called it a fiat—it would be the *Statesman* without the fizz. No *Statesman* reader would buy it.

Still others said it amounted to shedding the trusted, tried and loyal *Statesman* readership so that we could qualify to attempt wresting

Indlish readership from our contemporaries. One approvingly quoted the saying "A bird in hand is worth two in the bush".

The *Statesman* those days had two kinds of subeditors and reporters. One group, the minority but highly talented, provided the fizz. The other group, the majority, did the bulk of the work but were incapable of providing the fizz. The latter group continued to work as they had been working—prosaically, painstakingly, but unspectacularly. The minority, who gave the peculiar *Statesman* colour to the paper, decided to ignore the instruction. The result was that the Delhi edition of the *Statesman* continued to be produced as before, fizz and all.

In time the minority group withered away. One by one they were posted out or retired. I am not saying that this was done on purpose, but it did happen.

New Crop

The new crop of reporters and subeditors, trained in schools which give much less importance to the learning of the language, could at best manage straight English. At worst they were good at writing what the oldtimers of their category wrote, in other words *Indlish.* Over the next decade the *Statesman* tended to settle into the mould of the other English language papers of Delhi. It lost its distinctive character. The result is before us.

There are two lessons to be learnt from this story by students and practitioners of Advanced Journalism. One, it is not easy to change habits; and if you wish to replace a tried success formula by another, it is a herculean job, if not impossible. Kuldip Nayar had overcome resistance to change in UNI because it was by and large not yet a successful news agency when he joined it. Resistance in the *Statesman* was fiercer because people were unwilling to give up the special recipe on which the Delhi edition had thrived for decades.

The second lesson to be learnt is that mass communication is not as simple as it looks. Simplicity of language is basic to mass communication, yes, but it is not all. The target audience is very important. Would it be content with the cola, or would it insist on the fizz also? The *Statesman's* readers had for long got used to a unique mix of cola, fizz and colour. If one were to change the mix, one would have to find another audience, which is not easy in Delhi's intensely competitive market of English language newspapers.

Simultaneously with trying to get for the *Statesman* a wider audience, Kuldip Nayar's creative mind tried several innovations. He came up trumps with the weekly column, "I've a grievance, Sir."

It was not normal for the *Statesman* to pursue and seek redress for individual grievances. At the most a stray complaint from a reader about a wrong done by Authority would find its way into the "Letters to the Editor" column. Only if there were many complaints of the same kind—say overbilling by the electricity authority—would a reporter be detailed to investigate and file a report.

What Kuldip Nayar did was to invite complaints from staff members, friends and acquaintances of wrongdoing to individuals by public bodies. When half a dozen or more had been collected, he got them edited, complete with names, dates, addresses and specific complaints and published them as a local page feature under the headline "I've a grievance, Sir".

Stroke of Genius

Then, in a stroke of genius, he commissioned a reporter to investigate each complaint in detail and obtain the version of the other party. The investigation was to be done by telephoning, through personal meetings (if necessary by travelling) and by writing letters.

To the surprise of many, it turned out to be a masterstroke. Within days the wrongs done to the complainants were righted.

The reporter gave his report in each case saying the public authority concerned had blamed oversight or some other reason, apologised and righted the wrong. Many of the complainants came to the *Statesman* office profusely thanking the paper for doing what had seemed impossible to them.

Next week again grievances were collected and published along with the redress obtained in earlier cases. In time grievances, accompanied by photostats and other evidence, started pouring in and the reporter concerned complained of being overworked!

However, soon it was realised that, at least in some cases, it might be unfair to publish a grievance without ascertaining the other side's version. This "tilt" was righted by withholding the publication of a grievance until the other version had been obtained, then publishing the two together. The column was, therefore, renamed "Grievances" with a tailpiece called "Redress" published immediately below it.

This column was such a hit that virtually all the contemporaries of the *Statesman,* in Delhi and outside, emulated it. Today there is hardly a daily in India, whether published in English or any language, which does not have it.

Here is a story about the many-sided effects of this innovation in Advanced Journalism. One morning in 1972, as I was settling down to work an old, bent couple trudged laboriously into the *Statesman* newsroom. They were obviously weary and felt terribly oppressed. The story was that the old man had retired 10 years earlier as Accounts Officer from the Accountant-General's Office in Shimla but had yet to get his pension. In these 10 years they had spent all their savings. They had made many trips to Shimla but to no avail. Both were ill and obviously malnourished. They had no children. "Even if the pension comes through when we are no more, some distant relation will benefit from it. What use would it be to us?" The old man asked.

I forget the exact date, but this must have been late in 1972 or in January-February 1973, for there was a pleasant fallout of this for me.

I consoled the old couple, offered them chairs and tea, requested them to write out their story and provide any supporting documents which they had. This done, I passed on the grievance and documents to the News Editor.

'Pension Lost and Found'

Several weeks passed. I reminded the reporter dealing with grievances once or twice. One night when I was producing the main edition I found that the local page feature was "Grievances", and the top item had the thick three-column headline "Pension lost and found". I gave a quick up-and-down to the item (as all Chief Subs must do) and discovered that it was the old couple's case. The Accountant-General's office had replied that the papers had earlier been lost but had now been found and processed and the pension had been released!

I was excited and wanted to telephone the good news to the old couple, but they had no telephone. I went back to the gruelling job of producing the edition.

It so happened that I was in the midst of building my house and, to obtain a loan from the Delhi Administration, had deposited the original building plans, together with a copy, with the loaning authority. The loaning authority was supposed to compare the copy with the original and then return the original to the loan applicant by registered post. In practice this was never done. I too had not got my original plans back.

The day after producing the *Pension lost and found* edition, I went to the loan office to retrieve my original building plans. I needed them since the time had come to get electricity connection, for which too one had to produce the original building plans.

Brush With Bureaucracy

Radhey Shyam, the gentleman manning the table at the loan office, obviously the head clerk (by whatever name called), did not so much as look at me for five minutes. When I coughed and tried to tell him of my need, he cut me short by saying "not before April". When I tried to plead my case, he replied: "Look, in 1960 we disbursed Rs. 60 lakhs and I had five clerks; now we disburse Rs. 2 crores, and still there are only five. We are struggling to finish the accounting by the end of the financial year on March 31".

I pleaded with him that I was neck-deep in debt and repayment had already started. The only way was to move as fast as possible into the house I was building. This way I could leave the rented house in which I lived and use the rent thus saved to repay the loan. And, with the summer upon us, or almost, it was not possible to move in without electricity.

"Why?" he asked querulously.

I explained that even if I could rough it out without light and fan, the children could not. They were used to these facilities since birth; and they were to have their examinations in March-April.

He had an answer to this too. He lived in a house without light or power, or so he said. He was consequently not convinced of the urgency of my request. I tried to reason with him that it was the loan authority's duty to return the building plans, I came only because of the urgency. The man refused to melt. He had too much work for six persons, so... .

For some reason which is a mystery even now to me, the case of the old Accounts Officer crossed my mind. Luckily I was carrying the *Pension lost and found* edition in my hands. I spread out the paper before my tormentor, explained the old Accounts Officer's case and remarked: "Look, this pension was held up by the very people with whom the pensioner had worked for more than three decades; it was released only when he came to the public forum."

"So?" the man asked, arching his brow.

"My point is that Government servants do not always occupy the seat of authority, with the public standing before them like supplicants. There came a time when the Accounts Officer came to the *Statesman* office and stood before me just as I am now standing before you".

"So?" the man asked, again.

I drove home my point: "Don't you think that, like the Accounts Officer, you too may have to come to the public forum when your colleagues, senior and junior, have deserted you?"

"I see your point..."

He was stunned speechless. Regaining his speech after a minute, he replied: "I see your point, though I don't think any such thing will happen to me...Ram Din..."

Ram Din was the peon. He was asked to bring a pile of five or six files lying in an almirah. The one no top was mine. I took the building plans, gave him a receipt and a big thank you and came out.

Many think digging up scandals and improprieties is the hallmark of the distinguished practitioner of Advanced Journalism. They are only partly right. Agreed, this is a job worth doing. But there are other jobs equally important like using the media to get justice for wronged people such as the retired Accounts Officer and myself. Both these functions of Advanced Journalism—digging up scandals and getting justice for people—have the common purpose of serving the people. None of them is more important than the other.

As I walked down the stairs of the loan office and drove back home by scooter, I admired Kuldip Nayar's professional acumen. In his time he has broken many exclusive stories and dug up scandals. Many think this is all that needs to be said about Kuldip Nayar. The *Grievances* column shows him performing yet another important function of the Editor. The politicians and bureaucrats did not give him *Padma Shri* for this. The people and other journalists gave him a bigger honour by making the *Grievances* column, by whatever different name, a regular feature of all major newspapers in India.

Kuldip Nayar's *Statesman* was not merely *Grievances*. He did many things which students and practitioners of Advanced Journalism can learn about with profit. For instance, he was the one who started engaging full-time woman journalists for the paper. "What's wrong with them?" he asked rhetorically recently when I invited him to lecture to our students on Advanced Journalism, adding, "In fact there is much that is right with them. For instance, they are more dedicated and involved with the work—and this is my personal opinion and experience." A number of woman journalists recruited by Kuldip Nayar for the *Statesman* are now middle-level practitioners of Advanced Journalism.

Kuldip Nayar was also the first Editor in India to offer training facilities in science reporting—and a stipend—to students. Anil Aggarwal, now an environmental expert, was the first to benefit from it. He came during a summer vacation from IIT, Kanpur.

At Express News Service

A third function of practitioners of Advanced Journalism was highlighted during subsequent years when Nayar moved to the *Indian Express* as Editor of Express News Service. With his experience of UNI he reorganised ENS to give it more teeth. And it happened just in time because Mrs. Gandhi imposed the Emergency soon after.

Kuldip Nayar fought the Emergency in a way any practitioner of Advanced Journalism would be proud of. He devised ingenious ways to get his message across to readers of the *Indian Express*. When the news agency lines of the *Express* were cut, he got powerful radio receiving sets installed. A relay of stenographers were employed to monitor the BBC and other radio stations to get the world news. The correspondents of the *Express's* nearly dozen editions provided the domestic news. Such was the news coverage that few readers realised the *Express* did not have the benefit of the service of Samachar, the lone domestic news agency in which were merged the four functioning outfits (PTI, UNI, Hindustan Samachar and Samachar Bharati).

The worst part of the Emergency was pre-censorship, and Kuldip Nayar was one of the few Editors—one other was S. Nihal Singh of the *Statesman*—who thought it was a duty to communicate with readers despite the pre-censorship. How to do it?

Nayar used the time-honoured method of allegory. One article he wrote in the *Indian Express* was headlined: "No, Mr. Bhutto, No". The article berated the Pakistan leader for his dictatorial ways and for curbing the liberties of the people.

Though it was Mr. Bhutto and his misdeeds which were mentioned, between the lines one could see that the criticism was equally directed against Mrs. Gandhi's Emergency and pre-censorship. V.C. Shukla, her Information and Broadcasting Minister who was responsible for enforcing pre-censorship, took the hint. He phoned Nayar to say he knew what was meant!

Undeterred, Nayar wrote a second article. It was US Independence Day, July 4, 1975. The *Indian Express* carried Nayar's article giving extensive quotes from US history about independence, civil liberties, etc., including Jefferson's famous quote saying if he were to choose between the Government and a free press he would choose the latter. Again Mrs. Gandhi and her Emergency rule were not mentioned, but the hint was obvious.

Mrs. Gandhi's Government went into a flurry of consultations. What to do with this man who was openly berating the Emergency and the pre-censorship without saying it in so many words? The message was clearly going across to the *Express* readers.

Even while the Government was debating what to do, Kuldip Nayar wrote a third article. It was meant for students and tried to advise them what to do in life. The burden of the article was—be a doctor, be an engineer, be an administrator, be anything but a journalist.

Once again the message was clear. It was a crystal clear condemnation of the Emergency and pre-censorship which deprived journalists of all professional freedom.

Last Straw

This was the last straw. The Government could not allow Nayar to go on defying it. He was arrested and kept in detention. His wife Bharati Devi filed a *habeas corpus* petition in the Delhi High Court for his release. Two days before the judgement, Kuldip Nayar was released unconditionally after three months of detention. The judgment was, however, still delivered and the two judges comprising the bench passed strictures against the authorities. Both were penalised. One was transferred to Guwahati and the other, an *ad hoc* judge, was demoted.

Reporting for work at the *Indian Express* on his release, Nayar tried to figure out how to let readers know he had been released. The censors would surely not allow the news of his release to be published. They would also not allow any allegorical writing by him, having learnt of how devastating it could be. He therefore wrote a news item carrying his personal byline but talking of the weather.... "Today's weather is fine. The maximum and minimum temperatures are...and... The humidity is...", etc.

Word spread among *Express* readers and others that Kuldip Nayar was out and operational. The Government gave up. It was on the way to holding general elections. To rearrest Kuldip Nayar at this stage would be to give its opponents a handle to use in the elections. In a short time even the remaining restrictions were to be "relaxed", which meant they were not to be enforced, though they were not formally lifted. There was no point in rearresting Nayar.

We know what happened. Mrs. Gandhi's party was defeated in the elections. The Janata Party won. Kuldip Nayar wrote a book about the Emergency, *The Judgment,* which sold 100,000 hard-back copies.

CALLING ALL WOMEN?

Every paper nowadays carries a weekly section for women, or at least an apologia for it. Knitting, sewing, embroidery, home decoration and lately beauty care and much else are mentioned. The latest trend is to carry even intimate details, the sly calculation possibly being that it will attract male readers also, boys being boys.

However, the *Detroit Free Press* daily recently added a feature which is called the "Men's column". It is of course supposed to be read by men. But could it be meant to attract woman readers who might be wondering how to understand their men?

CHAPTER XII

Nihal Singh's Emergency

A mere two kilometres from the *Express* office is located the *Statesman* building at the confluence of Barakhamba Road and Connaught Place's outer circle. It was for three decades after independence a forbidding edifice for most citizens. Most people thought it was the preserve of the Brown Sahibs.

And not without reason. During the last two decades of British rule, it was the purveyor of the British point of view. There were two other English language papers in Delhi. The *Hindustan Times* projected the nationalist Congress point of view and *Dawn* the Muslim League viewpoint. With partition, *Dawn* migrated to Karachi leaving India's capital to the mercies of the remaining dailies.

In this background and with its non-Indian ownership until the mid-sixties, the *Statesman* seemed an unlikely candidate to fight authoritarianism.

Yet, it was much more than the voice of the Establishment or a fragile foreign-owned plant. It went by the highest norms of journalism. Accuracy was its watch word and credibility its creed. No matter whether it pleased or annoyed anyone, the *Statesman* refused to compromise on facts. Most of all, it refused to suppress news, no matter what happened. One of its earliest special correspondents, probably the first, was Durga Das.

Sneaking Admiration

Naturally, the *Statesman* was inconvenient to many people. Yet everyone had a sneaking admiration for this inconvenient and fearless purveyor of news.

In the aftermath of the debacle in the war against China in 1962, the *Hindustan Times's* S. Mulgaokar wrote a series of powerful front-page signed editorials topped by one headed "Not enough by half". This last piece was written the day Jawaharlal Nehru stripped V. K. Krishna Menon of the Defence portfolio following Mulgaokar's sustained campaign. Menon was left with the Defence Production portfolio. Mulgaokar's contention in the "Not enough by half" signed editorial was that it was not good enough to strip Menon of the brief to look after the defence of the country; he had to be sent packing into the wilderness because he had messed up the country's defence. Sure enough, it fuelled the revolt in the Congress Parliamentary Party. For the first time in his life Nehru was shouted down in the Parliamentary party meeting. Menon had to go.

The *Statesman* was still run by Englishmen who were not too sure if their views were in tune with Indian public opinion, though about news they were certain. The Editor of the *Statesman* was Alfred Evan Charlton, who specialised in enriching and imparting the paper's Communication Package. In his years as Editor he rarely wrote an editorial and never, to my knowledge, a signed article. He concentrated on getting the best out of his men.

Once when an Israeli dignitary visited Nepal, S. Krishnamurthy who was a Chief Subeditor in the Delhi edition of the *Statesman* went to cover the event for *Marriv,* an Israeli daily whose strigner he was. No Indian paper so much as took note of the event in its editorials because Israel was an international pariah for India.

Krish's Case

As Krish (Krishnamurthy's nickname) returned from Kathmandu, Charlton walked into the Newsroom. "Krish", he said, "I am told you covered the Israeli dignitary's mission to Kathmandu".

"He did, and he made a great job of it", I chipped in, having been shown the transcripts of Krish's many news telegrams to *Marriv.* Not only this, Krish had shown me the transcript of the three-part round-up of the Israeli mission's accomplishments which he had written on return to Delhi. He trusted my judgement and wanted his despatches edited by me whenever possible.

"Fine", Charlton replied half to me, half to Krish. Then, addressing Krish, he said, "What about writing an editorial about the Israeli mission's achievements and/or failures for the *Statesman?"*

Krish wrote the piece and it was duly published in the *Statesman*—the only Indian paper which editiorially mentioned the Israeli mission to Nepal.

I write all this to show what kind of paper it was which took on Mrs. Gandhi's Emergency in 1975. Appropriately, the man running the show was S. Nihal Singh.

Nihal Singh had been a subeditor working for the *Times of India* for a brief period before joining the *Statesman* as a young reporter. He had been brought up in the *Statesman* tradition with its almost disproportionate stress on propriety and credibility. He had been a fearless though careful reporter. After a time he became a foreign correspondent—serving the *Statesman* from London, Moscow, Jakarta and other world news centres.

11 a.m. to 1.30 a.m.

Nihal Singh was—or is—a man cast in the mould of Lord Krishna's man for whom "*Karma* is thy right, reward is not thy concern". He coveted no office. Yet, when Dilip Mukherjee who was Political Correspondent (Chief of Bureau in Delhi) left to join the *Times of India,* Nihal Singh who was posted in Moscow and G.H. Jansen, who was posted in Beirut, were shortlisted for the post. Both were summoned to Delhi. This was in May 1969. Nihal Singh, I still recall a quarter century later, seemed singularly unconcerned. He seemed ready to take on the new assignment, and equally ready to go back to continue reporting from Moscow.

In the event he was selected for the prestigious assignment. He became Chief of the Delhi Bureau (or Political Correspondent in the *Statesman*'s jargon).

And what a Political Correspondent he became! His next in command was K.K. Katyal. This was the time of the 1969 Congress split. There was never a day when Nihal Singh did not work until earlier than 1.30 a.m., though he started about 11 a.m.

I also noticed that he did not ever want to take news points for his stories from the news agency copy which some of us kept for him. He depended upon his own investigations. If there was anything which he had not investigated, he told us to use agency if we wanted.

Such was Nihal Singh's commitment to professional standards that when a scoop (exclusive story) of the highest order was brought to his notice, he refused to rewrite it; he insisted that we credit it to the source which gave the story first to us.

One fine morning (that is, 1 a.m.), Katyal came up with the story that the then Congress president, Mr. S. Nijalingappa, had issued a show-cause notice to Prime Minister Indira Gandhi asking her why she should not be expelled from the Congress for indiscipline. Nihal Singh's bland reply was, "Use it if you want to". Such was the integrity of the man.

Some years later, Kuldip Nayar who was the Resident Editor of the Delhi *Statesman* fell afoul of the proprietors (read Mr. C. R. Irani, Managing Director). It was known that he had been told to look for a job because the *Statesman* had no future for him. Nihal Singh was chosen to be his successor.

As was his style, Nihal Singh took over with the minimum of fuss. Since Kuldip Nayar, now designated Political Editor, was still occupying the Resident Editor's office, Nihal Singh got another room refurnished in accordance with the status of the Resident Editor and got going. None of us felt the crash of the whip. His familiar ear-to-ear smile continued to adorn his face. Yet he was effective and decisive.

Lunch Room Case

The *Statesman* has a Senior Staff Lunch Room where subsidised food is served by liveried and beturbaned *khansamas* to all the editorial staff and some selected officers from the other departments. It was essentially meant for the Englishmen and Australians who held the highest editorial positions earlier. More Indians came in but it continued to serve European food. Some Brown Sahibs from other departments also used it. With more Indianisation, grumbling started against "discrimination" which kept many non-editorial officers out. So, gradually, more of the non-editorial staff were allowed in. The membership swelled to twice the original figure and continued swelling. The *khansamas* grumbled. Their numbers had not increased but the work load was much heavier than before. The solution they suggested was an allowance to compensate them for the extra work, failing which they would work at their old pace. The result was that lunch hour which started at 1 p.m. and extended beyond 2 p.m., now kept going up to 3 p.m. or later.

This was something sacriligious in the *Statesman,* where everyone was supposed to work to time.

Nihal Singh thought the agitation was not in keeping with *Statesman* traditions. He arranged with Standard Restaurant on the first floor of the Regal building to serve food to the senior staff. The kind of lunch that we ate in our Lunch Room cost Rs. 9 per person per day those days at the Standard. So everyone was issued specially printed Rs. 9 coupons which he could trade at the Standard for lunch. The only condition was that no one was to go before 1 p.m. and everyone had to return to work and be operational by 2 p.m. Needless to say, the *khansamas'* agitation broke down after a few weeks and our Lunch Room again became operational.

Such was the man who took on Indira Gandhi's Emergency and pre-censorship on June 25, 1975. Various papers responded by inventing devices to beat it. The newspapers were supposed not to let the readers know that pre-censorship had been imposed on them. Some of the papers left blank spaces at places in their pages where news items or news points had been cut out by the Government's censors with the remark "not to be published".

The Government retaliated by issuing guidelines which made it clear that no white space was to be left and no indication was to be given to readers that anything had been cut out by the censors.

In an earlier chapter I have related how Kuldip Nayar in the *Indian Express* tried to bypass the censors to communicate with the readers of his paper. Nihal Singh, in the *Statesman,* devised his own formula.

The formula was ingenious. India gets heaps of foreign news from the multinational news agencies AP, Reuter and AFP, with which our news agencies UNI and PTI have tie-ups. About 50 per cent of the wordage received has to be killed by the editors of UNI and PTI at source because it has either no news value for Indian audiences or is much too lengthy for them. The rest is creeded to newspapers as edited.

Foreign News

At the news desks of the newspapers, more than three-quarters of the wordage received from the multinational news agencies cannot be used. Thus, about a page worth of foreign news, or even less, gets into the daily newspapers, including the foreign page and Page 1. The reason is that Indian readers are just not interested in Colombian politics or Brazilian road accidents, etc.

What Nihal Singh did was to issue quiet instructions to the Chief Subeditors to use foreign news received from AP, Reuter and AFP at length. Thus the *Statesman* started carrying detailed reports on accidents in Peru, agriculture in Brazil or the meat industry in Argentina. The foreign news coverage of the *Statesman's* Delhi edition swelled to more than two pages each day, sometimes more than three.

It was a brilliant move in Advanced Journalism. The Government's censors, partly because they were not too sure of themselves and partly on official instructions, cut all domestic news reported by the sole news agency Samachar or by newspaper reporters to the bare bonęs. I remember that hardly any item of domestic news sent by Samacher went to more than three or four paragraphs—unless it was the text of an official Government statement. News items filed by reporters of the *Statesman* and other newspaper were also cut down to the bare skeleton. If a reporter laced his news item with quotes from citizens or even officials, the quotes were cut out.

The reason is understandable. The censors were Government information officers who were more bureaucrats than newsmen. No one in those days wanted to take risks—and Government officers are always the least risk-taking. So the censors revived the old adage which had for long been discarded by journalists, "when in doubt, cut it out". Even if it was a fire in a market complex, the bare recital of the event was retained, the eye-witness description of how the fire started and/or how the fire fighters were lax was cut out.

The result was that not only political stories but news stories of accidents, fires, etc., were emasculated and reduced to two-paragraph or three-paragraph items. The total effect was a famine of news.

I and other colleagues in the Newsroom found it difficult to fill the pages. Even with photographs—which too were subject to pre-censorship—filling up pages was difficult.

Gaping Spaces

In such a situation we found Nihal Singh's directive to use foreign news at length very useful. One could confine local news to one page whereas in earlier days it overflowed to another page. The States and National pages were likewise truncated. The problem now was where to find news to fill the gaping spaces instead of struggling to confine an avalanche of news into a limited amount of space.

The biggest sufferer was Parliament news. Statements made on behalf of the Government in Parliament were given in a summary form. Even speeches by the Prime Minister and other Ministers were cut and pruned by the censors to ensure that only those portions of them went out to newspapers which would be good for the mental health of readers. Private members' speeches were censored even more drastically. A remark by a member eulogising a particular step of the Government would be used and the rest of his speech ignored. Speeches which were critical or tried to draw attention to inadequacies or mistakes were not reported at all. The cut and thrust of question hour and zero hour were just ignored. Thus a five-hour debate on a particular subject would yield 5 to 8 paragraphs, no more! Earlier, it was a job of skill to confine Parliament proceedings to a page and a half. Now we had not enough Parliament matter to fill even half a page.

A Life-saver

Thus stories of Brazilian accidents, the Argentinian meat industry and minor Peruvian earthquakes came to be reported at length in the *Statesman,* occupying two or more pages. In normal conditions, they would have not been used, or would have been cut down to a paragraph or two. In the new situation, they became a life-saver. For as everyone who has served as a Chief Subeditor producing an edition knows, the first job is to fill up all the pages of the paper and release the edition on time. The question of finesse, of packing the paper with news which will be read and relished by the reader, comes next. An edition released late is as bad as no edition at all.

I suspect that the Government's censors could not see through Nihal Singh's game. They could not fathom how the *Statesman* could fill up the paper without using all the items which the Government found desirable. Nihal Singh's formula was to use a lot of innocuous foreign news, thereby obviating the need to use all the doctored domestic news items which the Government got creeded by Samachar.

One advantage of using foreign news at length was that it could not be objected to by the censors. First of all, it was all creeded by Samachar after pre-censorship, so how could the censors object? Secondly, the Government was sensitive to the foreign reaction to pre-censorship. Not censoring or cutting down innocuous news of Brazilian accidents or the Argentine wheat crop enabled the Government to boast to the world that censorship was really not killing news but only filtering out passages which tended to inflame passions in India.

A bonus was that the *Statesman* those days had—and still has—an arrangement with *The Times* of London whereby we were free to take clippings from *The Times* (which we received regularly). In exchange, *The Times* was free to use the *Statesman's* reportage (though it rarely did; it used the *Statesman's* reportage as a tip-off source which enabled its reporters to build up their stories on India).

It was a long-standing arrangements since the time the *Statesman* was run by the British. Nihal Singh took advantage of this. The easiest way to tell the world that there was thought control in India was to stop news reports from *The Times* from being published in the paper, or to publish truncated versions of them.

To reduce a news item in size is a matter of skill. Subeditors are trained to cut or condense news reports in such a way that continuity is maintained. The effort is to ensure that the reader does not realise what has been cut and where.

The censors' cutting , on the other hand, tends to be the operation of a butcher. If a passage or paragraph is found objectionable, the censor just draws a red line over it and that's that. In such cases there are occasions where there is no connection left between the portion above the censored part and the portion below it.

There would have been a hue and cry in Britain if the censors had tried to cut stories from *The Times*. Britain is the west's sounding board for opinion about India. The Government of India is very sensitive about how the British press reacts to its actions because the world press takes its cue from the British press about India. If the British press, and more specially *The Times,* berated India for censorship, the world press—and therefore the world—would conclude that India was a fascist country where news, and therefore thought—were controlled.

Playing *The Times* Card

Nihal Singh is a very straight man. But unfortunately for the censors he is very intelligent too. So we were instructed to take large chunks of reportage from *The Times*. Earlier, it was common to lift only pieces which were of interest to Indian readers. While using them we would frequently edit out whole chunks which were of interest to *The Times'* British readers but were redundant for the *Statesman's* Indian readers. Now, with space being no problem, and in fact filling up space being a problem, we carried detailed reports from *The Times*.

Anyone comparing editions of the *Statesman* of those pre-censorship days with editions of, for instance, the *Hindustan Times* would notice the marked difference despite all the news in both the papers having been doctored by the censors. The *Hindustan Times* of those days would give the impression of being the Government's complete propaganda sheet. The *Statesman* would appear to have reservations about the Government's claims. Some key components of the Government's propaganda package would be missing, crowded out by the expanding foreign news segment.

I am certain many of the key Government censors felt foxed by the *Statesman*. The drill was that after all the news items filed by news agency and newspaper reporters had been doctored by the censors, one had still to send proofs of made-up pages to be passed by them.

Censors and Page Proofs

The Chief Sub of the *Statesman* would duly send bunches of four or five pages of the edition at night to the censors to pass.

If five early pages were sent at 12 midnight, one could expect them to be returned at 1-30 p.m. or later. We would promptly send 5 or 6 more pages—and they would be frequently held up for one to three hours.

Not only this. Often pages would return from the censors with one or two two-paragraph or three-paragraph items crossed out as "not to be published". One would have to fill in the gaps thus created and resubmit the page for recensorship. It was not good enough if the vacant space was filled up with a pre-censored item, one had to resubmit the whole page.

Most dailies suffered because of this delay. Readers expect their morning paper at 6 or 6.30 a.m. and if the paper comes later they may switch over to another paper which comes on time. The *Express* and the *Statesman* in Delhi were delayed frequently because they did not exercise self-censorship. That is, they would use whatever news items had been censored earlier, but had to replace them when the censors found them inconveniently placed.

Many of us, who were used to locking up the main edition about 2 a.m. and calling it a day about 2.30, were disheartened when the censors passed the pages at 4 a.m. or later. Some feared that the delay—the *Statesman* reaching readers at 7 a.m., 7-30 a.m., 8 a.m. or later—

would make our readership shrink. But Nihal Singh's perception as a practitioner of Advanced Journalism proved to be more sound. *Statesman* readers, aware of the pre-censorship requirements, stuck loyally to their paper. Though the circulation figure of a newspaper is considered confidential, to the best of my knowledge and understanding the *Statesman's* Delhi edition did not suffer any noticeable fall in sales because of the delay caused by censorship. Apparently, *Statesman* readers learnt to read between the lines to guess the real news which was not allowed to be published by the way their paper positioned the news. Or by the way it left our or included key news items. This was in contrast with how the papers which went wholeheartedly with the Emergency and pre-censorship treated the news.

Nihal Singh Replaced

Not able to cow Nihal Singh and the *Statesman* down, the Emergency rulers did what all authoritarian rulers do. They put pressure on the management to get Nihal Singh out of the *Statesman*. If that was not possible, he should be prevented from taking over as the Editor of the paper. He was the seniormost man and the editorship was his due. To its credit, the management refused to agree to both suggestions. Nihal Singh went to Calcutta where the *Statesman's* Editor is based and took charge of the position formally.

He was replaced in Delhi as Resident Editor by the less visible and lower-profile S. Sahay, who had earlier been working in Calcutta as Assistant Editor.

They also put pressure on the *Indian Express* to replace S. Mulgaokar, who as Editor-in-Chief was an implacable enemy of the Emergency. The replacement was V.K. Narasimhan, another less visible and low-profile journalist who was till now the Editor of the *Financial Express*. Not only this, Ram Nath Goneka, the big boss of the *Express* group, had his arm twisted and made to put K.K. Birla, who owns and runs the pliable *Hindustan Times*, on his Board of Directors.

There was an aftermath to the experience of the pre-censorship days which is worth relating. In early 1977, Prime Minister Indira Gandhi decided to hold elections. Though not lifting the Emergency, she announced that the pre-censorship rules would not be enforced strictly.

What did "strictly" mean? We tried to find out. One night I put the picture of a handcuffed statue of George Fernandes on Page 1 along with a story whose headline was, "Statue campaigns for Fernandes". The story was that George Fernandes was standing for the Lok Sabha from Muzaffarpur in Bihar, but since he was a prisoner (undertrial) in the Baroda Dynamite Case, his supporters were taking his handcuffed statue on a trolly to various localities to show how their leader was being persecuted. In the "relaxed" Emergency, the news and the picture passed the censors.

On another occasion, Sanjay Gandhi, who then was the big boss of the Youth Congress and was popularly expected to dictate to his mother Indira how many Lok Sabha seats his supporters should get, announced magnanimously in Jaipur that the Youth Congress was not claiming a fixed quota of seats from the parent party. The news, received by a long telegram from our Staff Correspondent in Jaipur, was for some reason considered so innocuous that the Chief Sub on night duty just held it over—that is, he not only did not use it, he never got it edited. He left it in the tray meant for unused copy.

Even more incredibly, the next morning's Chief Sub also looked at it (or must have), and instead of getting it edited and using it in his edition, just left it to the mercy of the Chief Sub at night (called the Night Editor).

I was the Night Editor. Every Chief Subeditor must look at all the copy he has inherited—to see which can be used where. I looked at all the trays and, sure enough, found the Sanjay Gandhi telegram in one of the trays.

Three Choices

The choices for me were either to use this story on an inside page (say States page), to use it on Page 1 with the picture which had been supplied by the correspondent, or to hold it over (not use it) as my predecessors had done.

I took stock of the situation. There were any number of routine stories which must have gone to all the other papers. Those I could handle and "place" in the paper. Every Chief Subeditor wants to use a few exclusive stories on Page 1 and on inside pages to give his readers a flavour unique to the paper. I decided to use the Sanjay Gandhi story on Page 1 because it gave a sensation of change. Indeed it refuted the rumour to the effect that a big chunk of seats would be allotted by the Congress to its youth wing. The Staff Correspondent concerned, Atul

Cowshish (now a Special Representative), had given a detailed account of Sanjay Gandhi's press conference. I passed on the long telegram to Suresh Prasad, then a subeditor and now a Chief Subeditor, with instructions to stick rigidly to the "no fixed quota" news point and cut out the frills.

Suresh did a good job of it. The long telegram thus became a short six-para news item focused on the "no fixed quota" news point.

Apart from the sensation of change, there was a design behind using this item on Page 1. All practitioners of Advanced Journalism know that to give to readers a Communication Package which gives, or seems to give, one side of a composite picture is unethical and erodes the daily's credibility. This was the day when Morarji Desai and Atal Behari Vajpayee had launched the Janata Party's election campaign at Ramlila grounds in Delhi. In the situation of a "relaxed" Emergency, we decided to report this at great length and as the main story (lead) on Page 1. The headlines were:

JANATA PARTY THE NATIONAL ALTERNATIVE
Desai and Vajpayee launch campaign

This, I visualised, was what the reader would like to read about most. Yet there was no comparable news from the Congress camp because Indira Gandhi was waiting to see what the opposition leaders did, and the smaller Congress leaders were waiting for her to tell them what to do. This was the result of years of cutting down to size of all Congressmen, so everyone waited to see what the big one said and then duly parroted it. If anyone had an idea, he kept it to himself.

In this new situation, specially in the context of the *Statesman's* two-year running battle with the censors, anyone could have inferred that we were tilting towards Janata if no news of Congress election preparations was carried prominently enough on Page 1. Yet Mrs. Gandhi and the Congress central leadership maintained a sphinx-like silence.

The "no fixed quota" item, two days old and with all frills edited out, was yet given VIP treatment by me. I had a big headline spread over several columns just below the Janata Party campaign story. The headline was—

NO FIXED QUOTA FOR YOUTH CONGRESS

The Resident Editor, S. Sahay, next day congratulated me for rescuing this two-day-old story and using it to such telling effect. Like me, he was keen that no one should be able to say the *Statesman* was settling scores by playing up the Janata campaign and not reporting the Congress viewpoint.

There was an aftermath to this which again has a lesson in Advanced Journalism for those on the production side. The two issues cited above ("Statue campaigns for Fernandes" and "No fixed quota for Youth Congress") were so successful that I repeated the formula again and again—looking for and finding news where no news seemed to exist. The other Chief Subeditors also got into the spirit of it. It meant taking calculated risks, trusting your judgement instead of sticking to the provenly safe path of using news items which everyone was likely to use.

Outstation Correspondents

One of the lessons which anyone who wants to be a Chief Subeditor, News Editor or Chief of Bureau should learn is this: care and consideration for a correspondent's efforts, specially an outstation correspondent's, pays with compound interest. Not only Cowshish in Jaipur and Ambikanand Sahay reporting from Muzaffarpur, but every outstation correspondent of the *Statesman* took heart from these cases. They bent over backwards and filed outstanding off-beat stories apart from routine stories because they knew there was someone to care for their stories.

Outstation correspondents of newspapers belong to a different class from local reporters and correspondents. While local reporters and correspondents are visible all the time to the production editors, and therefore are able to get their stories placed suitably, outstation correspondents think of themselves as Cinderella. After the first few months, they tend to think that whatever they file the desk would give them step-motherly treatment. Frequently, "play-safe" Chief Subeditors take agency copy on news events if their own correspondents' versions are even slightly late. The excuse is the deadline.

The fact is that the agency version of a news event is written for hundreds of newspapers in various languages in all regions of India. It is also used by radio and television. It therefore represents the GCF

(Greatest Common Factor). Whatever is not acceptable to everyone tends to be left out.

Another fact which few realise is that agency copy comes to newspapers edited. It is therefore considered safe by subeditors and Chief Subs. Often all that a newspaper subeditor has to do is to confine agency copy to the length his Chief Subeditor indicates. Which means lopping off the less important news points and retaining the more important ones and connecting the disparate parts to one another. If even after this there are complaints of poor editing, the guilt is diluted because it is shared by the agency subeditor. Indeed, I have come across News Editors and Editors who, while handing down a mild reprimand to their own subeditor for poor editing, shoot off protest letters to agencies. Since agency editors have no time to reply to such protests, the matter rests there. Everyone believes he has done his duty and the thing is soon forgotten.

The versions of a newspaper's own outstation correspondents are avoided not only by play-safe Chief Subeditors but by lazy ones also.

The *Statesman* always discouraged such laziness or play-safe attitude among its production people. But then the trauma of the Emergency and pre-censorship had drained enterprise out of most journalists in daily newspapers. Some in the *Statesman* had also fallen victim to this affliction. But the spirit of enterprise was always highly valued in the *Statesman* and it was difficult to drain it completely. Much of it was left among us, specially among the younger ones.

Bulging Circulation Figures

The result of the *Statesman* going in for exclusive stories of its local and outstation correspondents in a big way had dramatic results. Circulation went up by leaps and bounds. After being persecuted for almost two years because of pre-censorship, we were working with our tails up.

One day, while I was sleeping at home after night duty, an office car brought a message from Resident Editor S. Sahay. He had convened a meeting of all those taking charge of editions.

As we entered Sahay's office, he welcomed us with open arms and with a broad smile. He began the meeting by congratulating us for doing what he considered a great job. "Go on doing it the way you are doing. And just make sure to lock up on time, as you are already doing,

We are in for sunny times." Sahay had before him the latest circulation figures which showed a steep, perhaps unprecedented, rise.

Having been praised and pampered, we discussed how we could further strengthen the Communication Package we were giving our readers. Then we drank tea and went happily home.

That night I found that there was only one make-up man for the 16 pages of the main edition. There were four other pages of a subsidiary edition in which minor changes were to be made, and these also had to done by the same make-up man. Normally there are four make-up men for this amount of work, but some people had gone on leave and the management had not cared to provide replacements.

Possibly an oversight I thought, as I patted Francis, the lone make-up man, on the back. "Let's do it and show what we are capable of," I encouraged him. A capable man, he agreed but said I must write about this in my report.

Poor Brave Francis

After the edition, which was released bang at 2 a.m., I wrote in the report book "Only one make-up man for 20 pages".

Next night again Francis was the lone make-up man. Again he agreed to shoulder the entire burden, and again the edition went on time. My report read: "Good work by Francis, the lone make-up man for the second night running."

Incredibly, though the News Editor sent an extract from my reports to the Press Manager, I found that Francis was again the lone make-up man for the third night running. This time he was adamant. He had the feeling of being taken for granted. He had harsh words for me too. "*Aap ki kalam mein taqat hi nahin hai* (your report does not carry weight)."

I was furious at this callousness of the Press Manager and told the News Editor so on the phone. I agreed with Francis that he and I had both been wronged and if the edition was delayed we could not be faulted.

That night the release time was 2-40 a.m.—40 minutes late. I came back and wrote with my pen dipped in vitriol: "What is the use of telling the Chief Subeditors that they are doing a great job and must go on releasing the editions on time when the management cannot provide the minimum staff for the third night running?"

The News Editor and the Resident Editor put the management on the mat next day. As a result two things happened. First, when the Circulation Department sent a three-word note saying "Jaipur flight missed", the Resident Editor wrote on it "the Chief Sub gave ample warning" and passed it on to me to sign and return it to the Circulation Department.

The second development was that Tony, the very senior make-up supervisor who had retired only a few weeks earlier, was re-engaged on daily wages calculated on the basis of last pay drawn. He was told to come to work every night until I was satisfied that things would not go awry again. He continued to come to work every night for the next five months!

The significance of the "Jaipur flight missed" remark must be realised by everyone even remotely involved with the production of a newspaper. Those days there was a nightly flight to Jaipur about 3-40 a.m., reaching there in an hour. By releasing the edition at 2 a.m. night after night, we had built up a circulation of 6,000 copies in Jaipur. It took those days about 45 minutes for printing to start after the Chief Sub had released the edition. Thus, starting printing at 2-40 or 2-45 a.m., the *Statesman* was able to get about 6,000 copies ready by 3-15 a.m., when our van rushed to the airport to put the bundles on the Jaipur plane. With the edition released at 2-40 a.m. printing could start only about 3-30 a.m. and the *Statesman's* 6,000 Jaipur readers missed the paper.

It so happens that the daily newspaper is probably the only commodity in the world sold below cost price. Secondly, its shelf life is zero. Which means that we had first incurred losses by printing those 6,000 copies for Jaipur, and then had sold them as *raddi* (junk) by weight!

IN RAMA'S FOOTSTEPS

Lord Rama was banished to the forests for 14 years to enable his father to fulfil a vow. The Walla Walla (Wash) *Union Bulletin* banishes a reporter for one year to live, travel and work with a migrant Hispanic family. What does he find? He keeps writing a stream of reports for his paper. The Hispanics feel honoured by such a gesture, and the non-Hispanic readers know things about this minority of Americans.

CHAPTER XIII

Times of India Comes to Delhi

Running a thriving daily (or periodical) as its Editor involves a continuing exercise of the trade of Advanced Journalism. But starting a new paper or edition is, at the level of the Editor, pure Advanced Journalism.

I remember that when I joined the *National Herald* in 1959 I found a unique daily column called *Arrivals and Departures,* unique among all the dailies I had seen in English or Hindi. It had been started by K. Rama Rao when he devised the Communication Package for the paper as it was launched in 1938. In the thirties air travel was unknown and bus travel was for the rural citizens or the very poor. Everyone who counted in Lucknow, UP's capital, came and left by train. Rama Rao arranged with the railway station authorities to telephone the arrivals and departures of VIPs by train every evening. The consideration for the chore was Rs. 20 or 30 per month.

'Arrivals and Departures'

In 1959 the column was continuing because air travel was still rare even for VIPs except for Jawaharlal Nehru. The advantage was that if anyone of any value came to or left Lucknow, the readers knew about it. What is more, the *Arrivals and Departures* column gave a clue to the reporters of which VIP's visit to follow up.

D. R. Mankekar, when sent to the fledgling Delhi edition of the *Times of India* in 1950, made some daring innovations. The *Hindustan Times* and the *Statesman,* the two established English language newspapers of Delhi, had those days only one or two local reporters each. Mankekar plumped for six local reporters covering crime and courts, human interest stories and cultural and arts events. He also engaged T. Samuel to draw for Page 1 a daily pocket cartoon depicting the life, woes and joys of Secretariat lower division clerks who then formed the majority of New Delhi's population. "This cartoon feature was exclusively devoted to non-political and local affairs, civic problems and the people's small grievances", Mankekar said. The Delhi *Times of India* was thus the first among Indian papers to introduce the front-page cartoon!

Other contributions of Mankekar were a full-fledged foreign news page, a "News from the States" page and a local news page in addition to the commercial, sports and editorial pages. Each page was labelled appropriately at the top, a practice which apparently went out of use for more than two decades until it was revived in the 1970s by the Sunday papers and emulated later by the dailies.

To give exclusivity to the foreign news page, Mankekar arranged with America's UPI to give its world news service exclusively in India to the *Times of India*. In addition, he appointed staff or special correspondents in New York/Washington, Cairo (G. K. Reddy), Peking and Tokyo/Kobe (N. J. Nanporia), in addition to the existing correspondent in London.

Into Virgin Fields

As for the "News from the States" page, he noticed that while the *Statesman* cared for, and therefore circulated in, mostly Delhi and western UP, the *Hindustan Times* was sold widely in UP and Punjab, which then included Haryana, apart from Delhi. Instead of battling these two papers in their catchment areas, Mankekar decided to concentrate on the "virgin fields", as he calls it, of Rajasthan, Madhya Pradesh and Jammu and Kashmir. He reorganised the circulation machinery so as to ferry the *Times of India* on time even to small towns. For news he appointed staff correspondents in the major cities of these states and stringers (part-time correspondents) in the district towns.

Apart from all this, he would periodically send out roving reporter-photographer teams to the Indo-Pakistan border and other areas which he thought promised interesting news stories and features. These teams came up with some very interesting news items and illustrated features.

It was one such team, according to Mankekar, which unearthed the trans-border smuggling racket, including an organised racket in smuggling gold. Indeed, smuggling of all kinds of goods was "a major feature of human activity all along the border". Another feature of activity on the border was the operation of dacoits who committed the crime in one country and sought sanctuary in the other. It had apparently not occurred to anyone to investigate this possibility.

Among the human interest stories was one concerning a tribe which lived on both sides of the Sind-Rajasthan border, its members not knowing that India had been cut into two countries. Indeed, they seemed not to know of anything beyond Moghul rule.

Apart from sending teams of reporters and photographers, Mankekar himself toured these states, meeting Chief Ministers and other politicians and establishing links which over time yielded good and interesting political and other stories. He also made arrangements for local photographers to send news pictures to the *Times of India*, Delhi, on a regular basis.

One other assignment that Mankekar thought of was to send a reporter-photographer team to traverse the course of the Yamuna from its source at Yamunotri in Tehri Garhwal to its confluence with the Ganga at Prayag (Allahabad) 800 miles away. Though nothing dramatic was found, the pen and photographic pictures of the changes in the economic and social lifestyles of the people on the banks of the holy river over the years proved so compelling that a Chamber of Commerce financed the compilation of the reports/features and photographs into a book which was distributed free to the *Times of India* readers.

All this may look rather routine to laymen, as it did at the time to those running the *Hindustan Times* and the *Statesman* in Delhi. For instance employing six local reporters may look rather miserly today, when most Delhi papers can boast of a dozen or more reporters. But it required the vision of Advanced Journalism to think of it in the forties.

No Longer Country Cousins

And the impact was dramatic. The people in the states of Madhya Pradesh, Rajasthan and Jammu & Kashmir, long feeling neglected by the national papers, started thinking they had at last ceased to be the country cousins of the much-cared-for readers in Delhi, Punjab and UP. Those in authority at the Centre also started taking note of the trials and tribulations of the Madhya Pradesh, Rajasthan and Jammu & Kashmir people.

But most circulation centres in these states are far away from Delhi and receive editions produced between 5 p.m. and 9 p.m. the previous day. The sale of copies of the *Times of India's* Delhi edition in these three states could thus only be limited. The big thrust to circulation could only be given by Delhi and nearby areas.

Even in this the exercise of building up the "News from the States" page and reporting extensively from the Indo-Pakistan border, from the Yamuna basin and other "virgin" areas helped. After all, Delhi readers are interested not in Delhi alone. News of smuggling on the Indo-Pakistan border, for instance, has an all India-audience.

We have seen that the *Times of India* started out with six local staff reporters in place of the one or two of the *Statesman* and the *Hindustan Times.* That meant much more extensive local coverage than in the *Times of India's* contemporaries. Organisations, institutions and events like the New Delhi Municipal Committee, Delhi Municipal Corporation, local courts, the High Court and the Supreme Court (for each of which Mankekar engaged an advocate as a stringer), musical and other concerts, the arts, theatre, etc. got extensive coverage in the *Times of India.* A former ICS man who worked now for the British High Commission did the Western music critique. This man, named Kitchen, was an accomplished pianist, so accomplished that when Yehudi Menuhin once performed in Delhi he provided the accompaniment on the piano. As the concert ended, he wrote a review and rushed it to the *Times of India.*

Late But Fruitful

The Chief Sub at night had instructions to keep space for the review and for the picture of Yehudi Menuhin performing and delay the edition to carry it. As the review arrived, it was quickly edited and composed and proofread and pushed into the space reserved for it. Mankekar records that the edition was late that day and probably lost some circulation. But the *Times of India's* Delhi readers learnt that day that their paper cared enough for them to bring to them the very latest and best in news. It made for added credibility. Even those who did not get that day's *Times of India* learnt that their paper was late not because it was lax but because it cared for its readers.

All of us know what a force the *Times of India* is in Delhi today. Part of the credit must go to such care for readers which Mankekar and his successors took.

This has lessons for practitioners of Advanced Journalism which go beyond the norms of delaying the edition to take important news breaking late. One, the deadline, whether for news, for lock-up or for printing is flexible. You can take news which comes after the deadline and still lock up in time for printing to start when it should. Two, discipline in sending news to the press for composing is all important. If the press is fed news which it can compose well in time and the men and machines are free when the really big news breaks, you can get a lot of what is called "late news" into the paper without delaying the edition. The reason is that, though the subeditors and the composing machines and compositors are more than one (though never superabundant), the processing of the pages goes through a single channel. There is, in the case of hot metal technology (which is now being progressively replaced by photosetting), only one facility to flong all pages. Consequently, each page must take its turn to be flonged. If the flonging of a page takes, say, six minutes, and seven pages are sent together the turn of the seventh in the queue will come after it has waited for 36 minutes. If, however, the pages are sent at intervals of six minutes, no page will have to wait even for a minute. The same applies to plate-making and mounting on the rotary. (*See sketches on Production Bottlenecks, stages 1 and 2*).

The third lesson to be learnt is that the Chief Sub has done his duty only if he sends matter for composing in a steady flow. If he dumps all the matter on the press at 12 midnight, the composing machines would have been idle for hours before that time and will have a glut between 12 midnight and 2 a.m. It is thus possible to send all copy in a bunch to the composing room at 12 midnight and nothing after that and yet be late with the edition. On the other hand, if a steady and disciplined flow is maintained right from the start one can take news even after the deadline without delaying the edition.

I once sprang such a coup while working for the *National Herald,* Lucknow. Zulfiquar Ali Bhutto, Foreign Minister of Pakistan in 1964, had brought up the Kashmir issue in the UN Security Council whose meeting started only at 1:30 a.m. Indian Standard Time. Consequently the first take of the story, even with PTI making special arrangements, could not come before 1:40 a.m. IST. The lock-up time for the edition was 2 a.m.

What I did was to write three or four paragraphs of the history of the Kashmir dispute as ballast and get it composed well before 1 a.m.

I also ensured that all the other composing, proofreading and correcting was over by 1 a.m. By 1:30 a.m. all pages except Page 1 were ready, flonged, plated and mounted on the rotary. Even a trial run had been made on my instructions. At 1:30 a.m. four-fifths of Page 1 was ready, leaving only about 8 inches of space for the Bhutto story and a few more inches for the fillers which were also ready.

Reports of Bhutto's speech started coming about 1:40 a.m. and by 1:55 a.m. we had received five or six paragraphs. We got the paragraphs distributed on five machines so that within minutes the whole matter was composed. I proofread the thing myself and got it joined together with the headline under my direct supervision. By 2:05 a.m. page 1 was ready, by 2-20 a.m. it was flonged, by 2-40 a.m. the plate was ready and mounted on the rotary, and printing started about 2:50 a.m., which was 10 minutes before time!

Next day M. C. Chagla, India's External Affairs Minister, was to reply to Bhutto, and again the Security Council was to meet at 1:30 a.m. IST. This time I made more elaborate preparations. Apart from writing out the history of the dispute and a gist of Bhutto's arguments of the previous day (which were going in detail on an inside page), I cleared the decks for Chagla's reply to be carried as the lead story with a headline run over four columns. The reason was that Bhutto and Swaran Singh had had long negotiations spread over several months under the persuasion of President Kennedy and British Prime Minister Macmillan. The positions had consequently hardened, and Chagla was expected to do some plainspeaking.

In case, for any reason, the report of Chagla's speech did not come through, I had had a dummy lead story prepared, composed and corrected. The same story was reset as an ordinary single-column story in case the Chagla report did come through.

I got a scare when not a word of the Security Council meeting was received until 1:40 a.m. Consulting the rotary foreman, I found that all the other plates had been mounted and a trial run had taken place. Thus reassured, I waited.

At 1:50 a.m. PTI sent the flash that the Security Council meeting started on time. Another five minutes, and then the news came that Chagla had started speaking, calling Bhutto's speech a tissue of lies. He also condemned the Pakistani Foreign Minister for calling Indians "dogs". These and several other paragraphs were composed, corrected and kept ready.

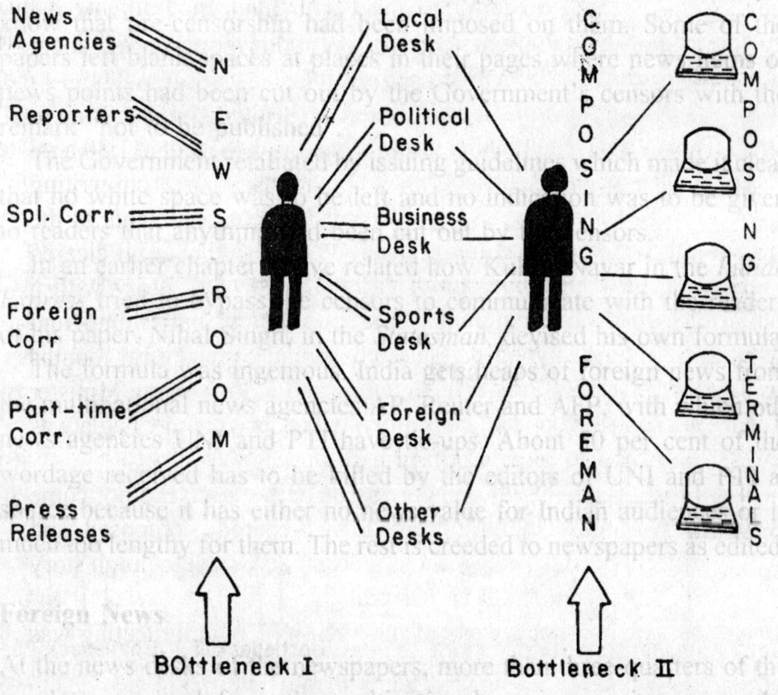
PRODUCTION BOTTLENECKS
Stage One
News Agencies
Reporters
Spl. Corr.
Foreign Corr
Part-time Corr.
Press Releases
NEWS ROOM
Local Desk
Political Desk
Business Desk
Sports Desk
Foreign Desk
Other Desks
COMPOSING FOREMAN
COMPOSING TERMINALS
BOttleneck I
Bottleneck II

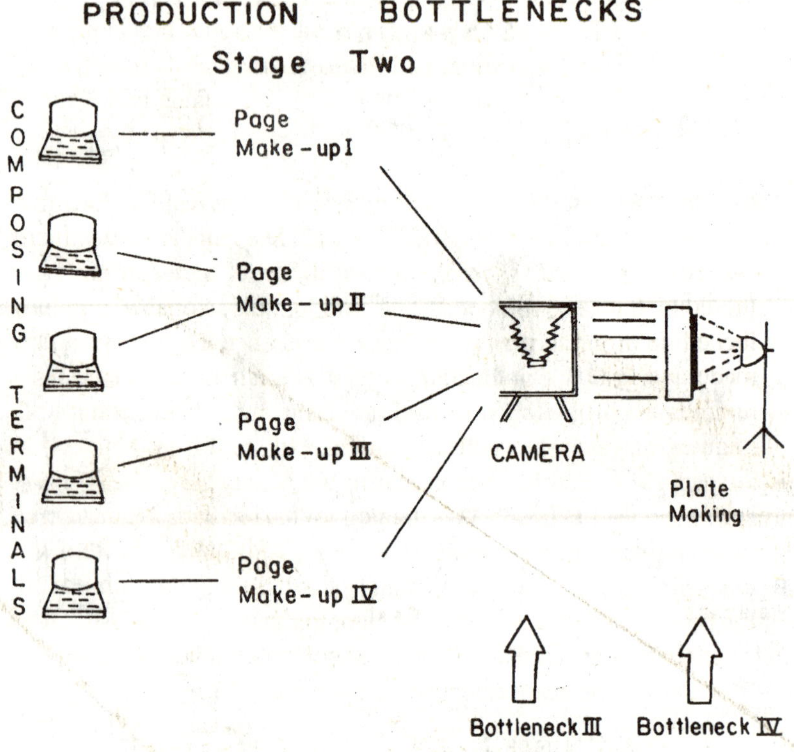
PRODUCTION BOTTLENECKS
Stage Two
COMPOSING TERMINALS
Page
Make-up I
Page
Make-up II
Page
Make-up III
Page
Make-up IV
CAMERA
Plate
Making
Bottleneck III
Bottleneck IV

At 2:15 a.m. came what I was waiting for. The news was Chagla's announcement that the context of the Kashmir dispute had changed completely and a plebiscite was no longer feasible. I rewrote this into the intro (or first paragraph) of the story, with other points following in logical order. Then I put up the following headline.

PLEBISCITE NEVER
Pak animus, not
Kashmir, in way
of amity
CHAGLA'S REPLY

This, incidentally, was the headline style we were following under the supervision of an International Press Institute expert who had come to advise us.

I kept consulting the rotary foreman, who kept reassuring me there was still time. At 2:35 a.m., he said I had now to lock up Page 1 or else the edition would be late. Within three minutes of this the page was locked up and was being flonged. So fast were the flong and the plate made and such was the advance preparation that printing started two minutes before time, even though Page 1 had been locked up 38 minutes late. All Chief Subs and production staff can take a lesson from this.

CHAPTER XIV

The Pioneer Story

In June 1984 I took two weeks' leave from the *National Herald,* Delhi, where I was a senior Assistant Editor, and went to Darjeeling for a holiday with my wife and two children. On the way back we dropped in at Lucknow for a day. While my wife and children met our relatives—her sister and the family and my brother and his family—I went on a round of the four English language dailies published from the city. I had worked in Lucknow for seven years—1957 to 1964—and expected to meet many familiar faces.

I did meet some old friends but it was a pleasant surprise to find two persons with whom I had worked closely decades earlier adorning the top two positions in the *Pioneer.* The Editor was R. D. Kwatra and the News Editor C. J. Baptista.

Kwatra had been the lone Assistant Editor in the *National Herald* in 1959. He also doubled as Consultant News Editor in the sense that if anyone had a doubt he could be consulted. The reason was that the paper had two very competent Chief Subs of about the same seniority, having worked in that position since 1946. To promote any of them might create discontent, or so it was perhaps thought. One of the two senior men was C. J. Baptista, the man who was now News Editor of the *Pioneer.* The other was A. P. Saxena (Piloo) who migrated to the *Indian Express* in Delhi in 1959 and retired as its News Editor.

Seniormost and Juniormost

It was Kwatra who had given me and others a test in 1959 and selected me for the lone vacancy. He was the seniormost man in the paper after the legendary M. Chalapathi Rau, and I the juniormost.

My association with Kwatra lasted not more than six months in 1959. I joined on May 6 and within weeks something happened which gave me a big opportunity. I recognised the opportunity and seized it with both hands.

The event was the gunning down by the Chinese in Ladakh of a nine-man Indian police patrol led by Deputy Superintendent Karam Singh. That same day there was rioting in the city of Kanpur which is only two hours' drive from Lucknow and nine people were killed when police fired to quell the rioting.

Chalapathi Rau wrote an editorial taking note of both developments in the very first sentence. Then he went on to rebuke the Chinese for what they had done and the Kanpur administration for letting a small incident snowball into a riot. He counselled moderation and patient steps to sort out things with the Chinese.

To us young people counselling patience was defeatist. Feelings had been inflamed all over India by the large-scale Chinese instrusions in Ladakh. For me the right comment by a daily of the stature of the *Herald*—remember, it was called prime Minister Nehru's paper—was a flaming editorial warning the Chinese and egging on the Government of India to deal sternly with them.

I could not digest Chalapathi Rau's editorial. Working on night shift, I stayed on and wrote a blistering piece which, if published, would have amounted to a declaration of war by the *Herald* against China. Then I put it in an envelope addressed to Chalapathi Rau, got his office opened and put it on his table.

All of the next day I was restless. Would the big man take offence? As the day wore on I became more and more convinced that he would. How could a slip of a boy be so impertinent as to pretend to advise the doyen of Indian Editors?

'God's in His Heaven...'

By the time I arrived for night duty at 8 p.m., I was convinced that the Editor would, at the very least, castigate me for poking my nose into things about which I knew nothing. At worst he might give me marching orders.

But there was an anticlimax. I took my seat at the horse-shoe table in the Newsroom. No one seemed to know of my daring deed of the previous night. People were laughing and joking. The Chief Sub for the night was clearing the decks for work. God was in His heaven and all was right with the world!

Ten minutes after we had started work, in walked Chalapathi Rau. It was usual for him to sit next to an old colleague and talk about things in general for a quarter of an hour or so before going home. This time he declined a seat offered to him next to a senior colleague. Instead, he walked towards me.

"Here it comes", I thought. But he took the vacant chair next to me and started a conversation. Where did I live? What did I eat? Did I cook or did I eat out? Was I married?

I answered the questions, wondering what was coming next. As the conversation proceeded, a doubt crossed my mind. Had he got my draft editorial at all? Could it be that the morning cleaning man had swept the envelope into the wastebasket?

The thought had barely come to my mind when Chalapathi Rau popped the million-dollar question: "Do you think your piece should be used?"

I mustered all my courage to reply: "That is why I wrote it". Would it be all right for the paper to counsel patience one day and stern action the next? This had not occurred to me, and I told him so. What if he used it not as an editorial but as an article on another page? Or in the magazine? It was up to him, I replied, taking heart, "you are Editor".

Finally the sweet-and-sour verdict came: "We will not publish it, but you have a talent for writing. I will give you a chance".

That started me, the juniormost journalist in the paper, on my career as a leader writer. I started writing two to three editorials a week and became one of the three members of an exclusive three-man leader writers' club. The other two were Chalapathi Rau and Kwatra.

Soon after this Chalapathi Rau was nominated a member of India's delegation to a Unesco session being held in Bangkok. He left a few stock editorials and told Kwatra he would send some more from Bangkok. Kwatra would have to hold the fort with whatever assistance "that young man" (meaning me) could give.

'Once a sub, always a sub'

I was unmarried and was infatuated with the profession of journalism. Indeed, I had become a journalist in defiance of the advice of my father, who had been told by someone of the saying "once a subeditor always a subeditor". My elder brother, an I.A.S. officer, pointed out that Editors did not retire, they only died. He pointed to Chalapathi Rau, S. N. Ghosh, Devadas Gandhi, Frank Moraes, Pothan Joseph and several others who went on and on.

Having defied such elderly advice, I had no go but to succeed. It was a life and death matter. Therefore, it was not unusual for me to work on an editorial in the morning, go out reporting in the afternoon and work at the desk at night.

This was in 1959. Before Chalapathi Rau could return from Bangkok, Kwatra got an appointment in the *Indian Express,* Delhi, as an Assistant Editor. He cabled his resignation to Chalapathi Rau, requesting to be relieved soon.

Chalapathi Rau came and reluctantly relieved Kwatra. Again there was left only one leader writer and I was again drafted to contribute two to three editorials a week apart from my other work. Of course there was no extra payment because in the atmosphere of idealism in which the *Herald* was born in 1938 and which it still maintained, money was a bad word. One was expected to work for the love of the cause.

Now, a quarter century later in 1984, I was sitting with Kwatra in the *Pioneer* office. Now 70, he had retired from the *Express* as its Resident Editor back in 1975. Then, he freelanced for 8 years from Delhi where he has a house.

Interesting Story

How he joined the *Pioneer* as its Editor is an interesting story. In 1983, aged 68, he received a message out of the blue from S.N. Ghosh, who was pushing 80. Ghosh had been working for the *Pioneer* in Lucknow while Kwatra was working for the *Herald* from 1938 to 1959. In 1946 Ghosh had become the first Indian Editor of the *Pioneer.* He retired in 1972 aged about 70 but was retained as "Advisor".

When the *Times of India* was about to start an edition in Lucknow, the *Pioneer's* proprietors became panicky. Ghosh's message was that Kwatra should come and take over the editorship and help the *Pioneer* meet the challenge. He himself was past the age when he could take on the burden. Kwatra accepted the offer.

The misfortune was that the *Pioneer's* subeditors and reporters had too long led a sheltered existence. The *National Herald* had fallen on bad days and was not coming out. The *Northern India Patrika* had failed to catch the fancy of Lucknow's readers. The *Pioneer's* journalists had therefore become complacent.

The *Patrika* had taken away a few of the better men when it had started its Lucknow edition some years earlier. Now the *Times of India* was luring the better ones among the remaining *Pioneer* subeditors and reporters with higher salaries.

Most of those remaining with the *Pioneer* were thus not exactly in a fit condition, mentally or by way of professional skill, to stand the *Times* challenge.

The strain on Kwatra must, undoubtedly have been great. Baptista, who was also past the age of superannuation, was to go for different reasons. Kwatra decided to leave too. He had been Resident Editor of the *Express* and Editor of the *Pioneer.* Further work as Editor, with all the handicaps and burden, seemed unrewarding to him.

Yet the proprietors were not willing to let him go until he gave them a "dynamic" senior journalist who could replace him. And, their experience was that such a journalist could be found only in Delhi.

Suddenly Kwatra broke the long recital of conditions in the *Pioneer* which he was making to me and popped the question, "Why don't you come?"

Fateful Letter

I was taken aback, I had worked with Kwatra only for those six months in 1959—and that was a quarter century earlier. I must have made an impression then. Besides, I had worked for the *Statesman* for 16 years, and it was well known then that no one could last with that hallowed paper, specially in the responsible position of Chief Sub, for that long unless he had real merit. This was specially the view in the *Express* where Kwatra had worked for more than 15 years.

Kwatra's question was most unexpected for me. Not able to give a straight "yes" or "no", I gave a diplomatic reply. "You are a guru-level journalist for me", I said. "I have to give the most serious consideration to this".

I took leave of Kwatra, sat for some time with Baptista who had been a colleague for five years (1959 to 1964) two decades earlier and returned to where I was staying in Lucknow.

Coming back to Delhi I forgot about the incident. Ten days passed, and then the mail brought a letter from Kwatra. It said the Managing Director of the *Pioneer* was coming to Delhi and I should ring up a particular telephone number and fix an appointment to meet him.

I went armed with some selected clippings of my writing. The

Managing Director, Shishir Jaipuria, refused to look at them, saying Kwatra had told him all about me. There were only two questions he asked. First, how much money would make me work for the *Pioneer?* Second, would I be able to meet the *Times* challenge to the *Pioneer* in Lucknow?

A figure was agreed upon as my salary. To the second question my reply was "yes" but on one condition.

I asked why the *Pioneer* was scared of the *Times.* The answer I myself gave was that the *Times of India,* which had started as a provincial paper in Bombay, had become "national" by starting an edition in Delhi. So had the *Statesman.* The *Pioneer,* which had, if anything, a more illustrious past, had remained a provincial paper because it remained in Lucknow. The remedy was to start a Delhi edition and give battle to the *Times of India* in the national capital. It would give the *Pioneer* the opportunity to cover Delhi news through its own journalists, which was what was making the *Times of India* a big draw for Lucknow readers.

The Managing Director listened most attentively to my arguments and, to my surprise, agreed. It was agreed that I would consult other senior journalists and prepare a project report to start a Delhi edition. It was also agreed that I would be Deputy Editor for a year to get a feel of how the *Pioneer* functioned. Then Kwatra would retire and I would take over as Editor.

The *Pioneer* Succession

Shishir kept his word about the succession. I joined the *Pioneer* on August 16, 1984, and succeeded Kwatra on August 16, 1985. However, about the Delhi project he developed cold feet. Two factors intervened. First, he was fearful of losses because he could spare only Rs. 5 crore for the project. How soon could Delhi stand on its own feet and start yielding profits? I told him plainly that instant profits in a newspaper venture were unheard of. The *Herald,* of which I had personal knowledge, had incurred losses from 1938 to 1961, when for the first thing it broke even. Besides, profits did not depend on the Editor alone. The Advertisement and Circulation Departments had a vital role to play.

The second factor was that the Pioneer Ltd. had obtained a licence for a security press which prints cheques, drafts and other such instruments for banks. A security press, Shishir informed me, yielded a 20 per cent profit from Day One. Unlike other Government contracts, printing by a security press did not involve the tender system. Work was distributed equitably among the few security presses in the country—unless any press annoyed a bank's management by not doing what it was expected to do regularly. The Rs. 5 crores had to be invested in the security press.

The decision to "delay" the Delhi edition—Shishir insisted it had not been abandoned—was made known to me in January 1986. I was told that the Delhi edition would come, but there would have to be a wait of four or five years.

This was not acceptable to me. I had prepared a comprehensive project report and devised what I considered a very attractive Communication Package after widespread consultations. While preparing it I had constantly kept in view the question why anyone reading one of the established Delhi papers would want to switch to the *Pioneer*. This indeed is a question which every Editor has constantly to keep asking himself. A delay of five years would most certainly render the Communication Package out of date.

Another reason was that while working in Lucknow from August 16, 1984, I had lived alone because my children were being educated in Delhi and I did not want to uproot them. I had led this uncomfortable life for almost two years in the hope that when the Delhi edition was started I would make my headquarters in the national capital. One could always find a dynamic man to be Resident Editor in Lucknow where the paper was entrenched. The Editor could make occasional inspection visits to Lucknow.

12-Hour Working Day

Since I had made a commitment to meet the *Times of India's* challenge, and partly because I lived alone, it was my practice to go to work at 8 in the morning and slog until 10 at night, or sometimes later. I helped the Editor by writing editorials. I also took it into my hands to direct the reporting and supervise the production of the paper. It was only when the first major edition—locked up about 10 p.m. for distribution in places like Allahabad—was through that I returned home. By that time all the major stories would be in and "placed' in the paper. The 1 a.m. edition, meant for Kanpur readers, and the 2 a.m. edition, to be distributed locally, took only the local news of these two cities plus any late news of national or international developments that came through. The steel frame being ready from the 10 p.m. edition, this was easy on most nights for the Chief Sub on duty. In case of an emergency when he could not decide, he could always ring me up, as happened on four or five occasions during those two years. On at least three of these occasions I had to come back to office at night.

I also worked a seven-day week in order to accumulate the weekly "off" days and visit my family in Delhi for four days once a month.

'Approximate English'

Not only quantity but the quality of work was also my concern. Uttar Pradesh having made English an optional subject at school soon after independence, the level of English of those who worked for the paper was at best ordinary. As someone* aptly remarked once, it was "approximate English". This handicap came on top of the complacency that reporters and subeditors had developed over the years because of lack of competition.

I could not change all this completely but could certainly improve things. The obvious thing was to concentrate on local and provincial news reporting, for that had to be the logical strong point of a daily which had been in UP since 1864 and in Lucknow since 1933. At the morning conference of reporters everyday we would quickly go over the "hits" and "misses" of the previous day. Then we would plan the day's reporting in such a way that there would be at least one major local news story for Page 1 and at least one for the local page. The coverage was widened in quantity also so that one page was no longer enough to contain the local news. In time we developed a second local news page.

I discovered that the *Pioneer* subeditors and reporters did not know how to write a news feature. Kwatra was too senior and too preoccupied with finalising the editorials and directing the production of the editorial page and the weekly magazine section to train them. In any case, it is not the job of the Editor (now often called Editor-in-Chief). This is something to be done by the Deputy Editor or the News Editor.

*Dr. S.N. Ghosh, first Indian Editor of the *Pioneer* (1946-72) and later an Advisor.

I took the job in hand. Once in a while I would rewrite a news report into a news feature if enough of facts and data were available or could be obtained. This went on the second local page.

The carnage following Mrs. Gandhi's assassination we covered fearlessly disregarding the possible ire of the rioters. When the first poster appeared on the city's walls decrying the killing of innocent people for what their co-religionists might have done, I wrote out a Page 1 story entitled "Delayed voice of conscience". The human rights group which had put up the poster reacted with satisfaction and its representative, Prashant Kumar, told me in graphic details how wooden-headed bureaucrats had put hurdle after hurdle in the way of the poster. It helped that Prashant, besides being a human rights activist, was a journalist working for the *Telegraph,* Calcutta.

Birth of a Feature

I converted all the information collected into a feature entitled "Birth of a poster" accompanied by imaginative visuals. The officials were furious that skeletons were hurtling out of their cupboards. Another news item giving more details was published two days later in the *Pioneer*. There was intense discussion among the officials whether this Deputy Editor from Delhi who was new to Lucknow (they were unware of my Lucknow antecedents) could be restrained. The all-knowing Premi and Chief Reporter V. K. Subhash told me of this.

I braced myself to face a term in prison. But someone restrained the furious officials. It would have created a furore if they had put the Deputy Editor of as hallowed and level-headed an institution as the *Pioneer* behind the bars. If that happened, reporters would go looking for more skeletons, and the other papers would join the hunt. I was fated not to have the unique experience of being imprisoned for writing fearlessly.

The *Pioneer* graduated to carrying a daily illustrated local feature and an occasional feature from one of the neighbouring districts, something it had never done before.

Editing local reports, which requires considerable skill and accuracy, was not the strong point of the *Pioneer's* desk. So I decided to identify and edit—sometimes rewrite—the local story meant for Page 1, the major story for the local page, and the local feature. I also monitored all the major headlines going on Page 1 and the local pages.

This was quite a job because one sometimes came across shattering ignorance of the language. For instance, when Satwant Singh was convicted and sentenced to death for killing Mrs Gandhi, one of the "senior" men overruled the Chief Sub and the subeditor concerned and gave the following banner headline:

DEATH TERM FOR SATWANT

I intercepted it just in time and gave the more prosaic headline:

SATWANT SENTENCED TO DEATH

Some days later, when the Supreme Court was conducting hearings for the possible confirmation of the death sentence, it found certain flaws in the documents submitted and returned them to the High Court for resubmission after correction. It specifically stated that it was giving no opinion on the question of confirmation of the sentence, which it would consider after the corrected documents had been submitted to it. The same "senior" person gave the following headline, overruling the Chief Sub and the subeditors:

SATWANT'S DEATH SENTENCE NOT CONFIRMED

I intercepted and changed this also because it gave the impression that the Supreme Court had rejected the High Court verdict.

The *Times* tide had been halted but not rolled back. It clearly needed a bigger push. The occasion came soon.

Satyapal Premi, *India Today's* correspondent in UP, was a dear professional friend who gave me tips about stories of strictly local interest in which his fortnightly was not interested. One day, while going on his news-gathering round by scooter, he found pulpits and other structures being constructed in Begum Hazart Mahal Park in the heart of Lucknow. What for? He made inquires and met A.K. Braroo, an officer from the Song and Drama Division of the Union Information and Broadcasting Ministry. Braroo said the proposal was to hold a light and sound show of the kind run at Delhi's Red Fort. This was to honour Begum Hazrat Mahal, consort of the Nawab of Oudh, who had fought the British during the 1857 War of Independence with a handful of followers when the regular army and Generals had fled.

I made further inquiries from Braroo and wrote out the story which was displayed prominently on Page 1. All of Lucknow was agog at the prospect, specially the senior citizens who had an idea of what a freedom struggle was like. Such was the sensation of change created that the *Times of India* and other contemporaries carried the story, or another version of it, sheepishly the next day.

For the next few months we carried reports on the progress of work at the Begum Show once a week or so. I struck up a close friendship with Braroo and made others working on the project news sources. It became my personal beat.

Suddenly work on the project stopped. Why? I made inquiries and discovered that Braroo had also left suddenly one night! It was becoming curiouser and curiouser.

Pre-emptive Strike

The mystery required inquiries from the very beginning. Who initiated the project? The UP Government made the request to Delhi and the Song and Drama Division started it. Why was work abruptly stopped? Because the Nagaland Government had made a pre-emptive strike and got the Central Government to direct the Song and Drama Division to divert the special lighting and other equipment to a project on its territory. The diversion was done at the political level.

Apparently, the UP political leadership—mainly N. D. Tewari who was then Chief Minister—did not bother as much as the Nagaland leadership. It had not seen it fit to stand up for its baby.

It was not my case that Nagaland should not get a sound and light show. But almost half a lakh had been spent on preparations for the Begum Show and it could be completed in another fortnight or so. After holding the show for a month or two, the Song and Drama Division could take the equipment to Nagaland or anywhere else.

When I made inquiries in Lucknow, the UP leaders pretended that they had nothing to do with the Begum Show. It was a Government of India project.

Coming to Delhi, I contacted the concerned officials who were piqued why the UP leaders should disown something which they had actually done. This was the chink I needed. I plugged at it with all the reporting and PR ability I had. The officers finally opened the files before me. Sure enough, the UP leaders had meekly acquiesced in the shelving of the Begum Show.

I broke the news on Page 1 of the *Pioneer*. A week later, I came up trumps. It was by now April 1985. If the Begum Show did not begin in another month, UP's torrential monsoon rain would start and wash out all that had been done. It was therefore no longer a question of the shelving of the project but of its abandonment. Besides, all the money spent on the project would be a dead loss and the park in the heart of the city could remain disfigured because there was no provision for clearing the debris.

The story had now become a public interest campaign, the first of a series. Pressure was brought to bear on me to discontinue it.

Most surprisingly, the Managing Director, Shishir Jaipuria, allowed himself to be made the instrument of this pressure. He asked me why I was after the Begum Show and advised me to discontinue it. I pointed out that it was such reporting on local issues which was helping the *Pioneer* meet the *Times* challenge. Local reporting had to be our strong point just as national and international reporting was the *Times of India's*. Succumbing to such pressure amounted to surrendering our main weapon. Either the campaign continued or I would quit. Shishir relented.

Though I trod on many toes, the campaign was successful. Work on the project was resumed and the Begum Show was seen by thousands of Lucknow citizens.

Last Show

A glittering array of citizenry was invited to the last show. I was also invited. As I reached there, whom did I see but Basu Bhattacharya, Bimal Roy's ace cameraman and now a film director! He had come to can the show on video for posterity!

I interviewed him quickly and drove back to the *Pioneer* Newsroom. It was 11-30 p.m. Could the Chief Sub take an exclusive six-inch story on Page 1 for the Lucknow edition? C. K. Mukand, the Chief Sub (now News Editor), gamely agreed. I typed out the story which began thus:

"The Begum Show seems destined to go down in history in a blaze of glory. Minutes before the last show was about to start flew in Basu Bhattacharya this evening. The ace cameraman and director announced that the Government of India had commissioned him to can the show for posterity...."

The vastly expanded local reporting with quality being monitored by me personally, the quest for exclusive stories and to top it all the public interest campaigns like the Begum Show had enabled the *Pioneer* to breathe more freely. Circulation and advertising revenue were again going up.

But this had brought to the fore claims for recognition from unexpected quarters. There was the Additional General Manager, Prem Kumar Rastogi, who wanted to start a badly written but well thought out column on business. Then there was the new Works Manager named Tapash Ghosh.

I had known Tapash from my *Statesman* days. He was the son of the *Statesman's* Rotary Engineer in the sixties. The *Statesman* had sent Tapash at its own expense to be trained at *The Times's* press in London. On return he had become Rotary Machine Minder (Foreman). Later he migrated to the *Pioneer*, then further east to the *Amrita Bazar Patrika* in Calcutta and now back to the *Pioneer.*

Tapash started thinking of himself as the big technical expert who made the difference. He advised me to arrange classes for subeditors and reporters on the new technology. He would make them wise about the new magic.

I was not averse to getting the subeditors and reporters to hear him. But for some reason or the other no lectures could be held for some weeks. He started telling common friends it was his technical expertise which was making the difference.

When I shrugged off the stories coming from these common friends, he started putting hurdles in my way. Bromides from the photosetting room were no longer to be taken to the Newsroom. If the Chief Sub or the Deputy Editor wanted to see them, they had to come to the composing room which was a flight of rickety wooden stairs down from the Newsroom. Secondly, it was decreed that anything composed had to be used because composing was a costly process. Thirdly, if the Deputy Editor wanted to get a headline or the make-up of a page changed, he could not do so. Why did he not think of it earlier?

Resignation

This was in July 1985. It had taken me 11 months to steady and improve Page 1, the local page and the features page (or the second local page). Now I planned to take on the job of detailed and planned revamping of the other inside pages. This opportunity was being denied to me.

I wrote to the Managing Director that such revamping was the logical next step in the development of the paper. If it was not to be allowed, if the work of the Chief Sub or a subeditor could not be reviewed and if necessary changed by the Deputy Editor, where was the point in having this functionary? Hence I was resigning.

I submitted this letter just before coming to Delhi for my monthly four-day visit. I had told no one but Premi.

Premi watched silently as the Managing Director and the General Manager frantically sent messages to the senior journalists of the *Times of India* and the *Patrika* that the News Editor's post (not the Deputy Editor's) was available in the *Pioneer.* They probably thought they would make do with a News Editor instead of a Deputy Editor, who is senior and has to be paid more. When they started interviewing people, Premi told everyone what had happened.

When I returned from Delhi four days later, all the journalists of Lucknow looked at me with admiration. Here was a man who could sacrifice his job for professional excellence.

Meanwhile the General Manager and the Managing Director went to Delhi looking for a replacement for me. They couldn't find anyone willing to come under these circumstances.

A few days after I had returned, the General Manager held a conference with me. He told me they could find no replacement and hence I would have a free hand. Not only this, Kwatra, who was already in Delhi and was unwilling to return unless compelled to do so, would retire as scheduled and I would succeed him on August 16, 1985.

I did, and made great efforts to complete my project report and Communication Package for the Delhi edition. However, as narrated earlier, in January 1986 came the bombshell of the shelving of the Delhi edition. I was no longer interested in working for the *Pioneer* and told Shishir so. Late in March 1986 I came back to Delhi to launch the Delhi edition of Bombay's *MID-DAY.*

CHAPTER XV

Telegraph Magic

The biggest daily in the Bengali language is *Ananda Bazar Patrika*. It once started the *Hindusthan Standard* in English to rival the *Statesman* in Calcutta. And, following the dictum that you should carry the battle to the enemy camp, it started an edition in Delhi. But it could not shake the *Statesman* either in Delhi or in Calcutta. Both editions of the *Hindusthan Standard* consequently closed down in the early 1960s.

What was wrong with the *Hindusthan Standard?* Nothing, if one went by conventional standards. It carried all the news like every other daily. It had all the columns too. It spent money lavishly and had some very capable journalists on its staff.

What it lacked was someone who would try to answer the troublesome question, "Why should anyone switch over from the *Statesman* to the *Hindusthan Standard?"* In other words, it had enough of skilled journalists but not enough of practitioners of Advanced Journalism who had the skill and knowledge to give the right answers and key decisions and take the right initiatives.

When the *Hindusthan Standard's* Calcutta edition folded up, it had a weekly magazine-size stitched supplement which was distributed free with the Sunday paper. It was called simply *Sunday* and carried several innovative features, including the gossipy *Khas Baat.*

Birth of *Sunday*

Though the *Hindusthan Standard* was closed down, *Sunday* blossomed into a full-fledged weekly magazine. The man who brought about the transformation was M.J. Akbar.

Akbar had been a learner in Khushwant Singh's *Illustrated Weekly* when it was climbing new peaks of popularity. A fundamentalist thinker himself he had learnt the value of calculated iconoclasm.

Though the *Hindusthan Standard* had folded up, the itch to have an

English language rival to the *Statesman* remained. Akbar, with his credentials established with *Sunday* magazine, was therefore the man to run an English daily when the *Ananda Bazar* group decided to have another fling.

The new daily was the *Telegraph.* And what a success it became! Like Kuldip Nayar's three-point formula for UNI, Akbar had devised a deceptively simple success formula for the *Telegraph.*

To begin with, he decreed that he did not want experienced journalists for his paper. At an Extension Lecture for students of the Indian Institute of Mass Communication in Delhi, he explained why. People who have worked for a few years as subeditors and reporters tend to have set habits of working based on their initial experience. Akbar wanted to inculcate a new kind of work culture among them.

Prashant Kumar, the *Telegraph* correspondent in Lucknow, once told me that his paper insisted on him filing full reports on everything going on in his beat even if he could find nothing exclusive. If the Chief Minister held a press conference, Prashant must report it no matter whether his paper used it or not and even if he was able to cover only that ground which the news agencies were to cover. The Chief Subs in the *Telegraph* Newsroom were simultaneously instructed to prefer staffer reports to agency, if necessary by waiting for them.

Looks simple? Even wasteful? Expensive it might be because all the outstation correspondents would be filing dozens of telegrams daily, but not wasteful. Apart from the telegraphing cost, transport costs a lot for reporters and correspondents who are expected to scurry from place to place looking for and reporting news.

1,200 Telegrams a Day

However, if it looks simple, the looks are deceptive. If a hundred correspondents filed a dozen telegrams a day, there would be 1200 staffer news items for the Chief Subeditor to choose from. This is apart from the hundreds of news agency reports.

Contrast this with what happened in the *Statesman.* The *Statesman* philosophy is that its correspondents, specially the senior ones, file a report only when they can find something exclusive, or at least a new angle to a routine story. If there is nothing new, the Chief Sub is expected to use the agency news story.

The result of this new approach of the *Telegraph* was that, while its journalists slogged for long hours reporting what could turn out to be routine stories, and while many such stories could just not be accommodated and many more had to be drastically edited to confine them to the length which the space constraint permitted, all the *Telegraph* reportage had a new look and freshness unique to itself. Frequently, the *Telegraph* reporter would write a news story from an angle which looked most normal to him but which turned out to be very different from the angle taken by the reporters of the news agencies—PTI and UNI. Thus, news items which were reported by UNI and PTI and published as such by the papers looked like exclusive when reported by correspondents of the *Telegraph.*

A second *Telegraph mantra* was to carry all the news items which had to be carried for record purposes as brief skeletonised items in a single column on Page 1, leaving the rest of the space on the page for the display of special stories.

Which meant what? While the *Telegraph* carried all the news which had to be carried to inform the readers of the day's developments, the whole paper gave the impression of being full of exclusive stories, or at least of exclusive angles to routine stories.

Now, newspaper production is the business of creating an image. Theorists of mass communication are fond of saying that perception is reality—I learnt of it from Dr. J. S. Yadava, Director of the Indian Institute of Mass Communication, in 1991. Similarly, a newspaper is only as exciting or "newsy" as the image it creates on the mind of the reader. If the reader thinks today's newspaper is dull, it *is* dull. No Editor is going from door to door to explain to the reader that our paper is not dull, that we are carrying all the news that our contemporaries are carrying plus some more which they are not carrying. On the other hand, if the reader does think today's edition is newsy, it has got to be newsy no matter which, and how many, stories it misses.

Exclusive Look

The *Telegraph's* strategy of insisting that its correspondents cover whatever news events were worth covering in their opinion ensured that all—or most of—its new stories had an exclusive look. The sensation of change was there and this is what the reader cares for.

A second rule of thumb which Akbar told us of in his Extension Lecture was to let no news story continue from page 1 to an inside page.

He explained how. If a correspondent filed a long story, and assuming that more of it was worth carrying than could be accommodated on Page 1, you cut it up into two. Carry the part you think should go on Page 1 on that page and reintroduce the rest and carry it inside. This is a simple enough exercise as every subeditor knows. What is important is to carry a pointer on Page 1 with the main story to show on which page all the other juicy details of the story are going. This will rid the reader of the trouble of locating where the run has gone.

Secondly, while reading one story of his choice on Page 1, he gets the sensation of reading another story whose pointer he reads along with the main story. Thus if he reads seven news stories on Page 1 with pointers to five other stories on inside pages, the image on his brain is of 12 news stories, whereas he has read only 7 news stories and 5 pointers.

Stroke of Genius

It was a stroke of genius. People all over India started thinking the *Telegraph* was a very newsy paper. Small and big towns all over the country made a demand for a few hundred to a few thousand copies of the *Telegraph* each morning even if it reached one day late. Such was the freshness Akbar's magic formula imparted to the paper.

Circulation figures are normally considered confidential. But if they are analysed for the *Telegraph* for the initial years, they will show that it became the very first daily in the past few decades to spread its circulation over a very large number of towns and cities. In the case of other major dailies, the bulk of the circulation comes from a cluster in and around the place of publication. In the other towns and cities circulation is only sparse. If ever there was a truly national daily in India, it was the *Telegraph,* though many papers lay claim to that title.

The third prong of the *Telegraph's* success formula is featurised reporting. The tight editing of most spot news stories, pruning them of flab and leaving only the skeleton, meant more space for featurised reporting of selected news stories of special significance.

The biggest tribute to the *Telegraph* magic formula is the extent to which it is being sought to be emulated.

The *Indian Post,* after the initial phase of S. Nihal Singh's editorship, turned to the new formula and became an eminently readable paper, though it could not break the stranglehold on the Bombay market of the *Times of India.* Such was the spell of this formula that a whole newspaper called the *Independent* was created to exploit it. Finally has come the Delhi edition of the *Pioneer,* a daily for which I had visualised and prepared the initial project report in 1985-86. It now follows the formula followed successively by the *Telegraph,* the *Indian Post* and the *Independent.*

Even the old, established dailies, specially their Sunday editions, are trying to mould themselves according to this formula. The most obvious example is the *Times of India's* Sunday edition, now renamed the *Sunday Times of India.*

INVOLVING THEM ALL

Newspapers are no longer merely a compilation of news or of editorial wisdom. They are, or ought to be, "the friendly neighbourhood sage, sympathiser and adviser", according to an observation on the media in the weekly *Sunday.*

The *Lokmat Times* of Aurangabad (now also Nagpur) brings out two pullouts every alternate Friday, one for children (classes V to X) and the other for the youth (college students). Both pullouts are the handiwork of students themselves led by their Principal, with technical help from the newspaper's journalists and other staff.

The response is such that the *Lokmat Times* wants to make the pullouts a weekly feature. It involves children and youth with the paper as nothing else.

Whose brainchild? Naturally Executive Editor Alok Varma's.

LESSONS FROM CASE STUDIES

CHAPTER XVI

The Smile and Advanced Journalism

Nine case studies have been given in earlier chapters of this book. One thing common among all the personalties involved is that all of them are (or were) great smilers. None of them was or is a frowner. Here is the rationale of the smile as an essential ingredient of Advanced Journalism.

Each person has one father and one mother. Assume that each person has four siblings. There will be anything from 50 to 200 close relations and 100 to 500 distant relations. Over your school and college career you may have known 200 to 500 classmates and schoolmates. Up to now you may have known 500 persons living in your neighbourhood. You may also have some 2000 acquaintances whom you may have met for 5 minutes to 2 hours at public or private functions. The total for the average person comes to the following:

Father	1
Mother	1
Siblings	4
Close relations	200
Distant relations	500
Class and schoolmates	500
Neighbours	500
Acquaintances	2000
Total	3706

For particularly gregarious persons the figure may go up to 5000 or more. For those who are generally reticent and withdrawn it may come down to 2000. Here is how we can harness this essential resource to the maximum advantage of a journalist:

1. *Drop in the Ocean:* Delhi has a population of 138 lakhs. Your state may have a population of one crore to 20 crores. India has a population of 100 crores. The world has a population of several hundred crores. Thus, the number of people with whom any individual has links (2,000 to 5,000) is like a drop in the ocean.
2. *Preservation:* Each of us during a lifetime acquires the acquaintance, friendship, love of or other kinds of links with 2,000 to 5,000 persons. This includes one father, one mother, a few siblings, present and former classmates, present and former colleagues and neighbours, chance acquaintances whom you run into at weddings and other public and private functions, and anyone whom you have known at any time in life. These links must not be allowed to be broken or weakened. They must be strengthened.
3. *Promotion:* It is necessary to promote people from a lower category to a higher category. For instance, distant friends should be promoted to close friends, distant relatives to close relatives, etc.
4. *Widening the circle:* It is plain common sense not only to preserve established links, strengthen them and promote people from a lower category to a higher one, but to widen the circle. This means making an effort to meet new people, cultivate them, make friends with them. The Americans call this being "good mixers".

The smile is an important, perhaps the most important, catalyst in getting life's work done. But in the media it is absolutely vital, both in reporting and in production. This is because information becomes news only when it relates to man, now or potentially. Animals, even inanimate objects, become news when they relate to man, actually or potentially.

How it Works

In news gathering, or reporting as it is called, one has to have sources. There can be no news without sources. A successful reporter keeps in touch with his sources, even if he does not need to get news from them immediately. This is because the reporter is much more likely to get his source's cooperation when he keeps in touch; if the goes to the source only when he needs information there is much less likelihood of cooperation.

The smile is the cheapest, least time consuming and by far the most cost effective way of keeping in touch. Going into his news beat, the reporter is likely to run into news sources he does not need immediately. Just a smile and a hullo strengthens the bond as nothing else. On the other hand, if the reporter ignores a source because it is not needed immediately, he will find the source uncooperative when the need arises.

Variants of the smile are—greeting cards, telephone calls even when one is not looking for news, maybe an occasional letter, a greeting on a joyful occasion (wedding, birth of a child) and, most importantly, a show of solidarity and support on a sorrowful occasion.

Production

Newspaper production is team work. No matter how good or mediocre a member of the team is, he has a role. Also, no matter how small a job he does. Smile at him, and keep smiling day after day, and he will do his bit willingly; often he will do things "above and beyond the call of duty" as the army says. Frown at him, or ignore him because he is "almost insignificant" by way of his contribution to the team effort, and he will sulk, sometimes cite hurdles which he would otherwise remove, find excuses, or just go out for a cup of tea.

As shown earlier, people whom we know can be divided into four broad categories:

A. *Those who are close to you by blood relationship or otherwise:* Smile at them, and they will warm up to you; don't smile at them and they will feel taken for granted.

B. *Those who know you a little and may or may not remember your name or where you met:* Ignore them, and the tenuous link will snap; smile at them and they will feel closer. If any of them remembers you by face but not by name, or does not remember where and why you met, the smile will make him rack his brain to remember the missing link. You have made him take time off his other preoccupations to think about you. A second such occasion, and he will start feeling closer to you.

C. *The third category consists of those who may have a vague feeling that they have seen you somewhere:* Ignore them, and they will dismiss you from their thoughts as an illusion; smile at them and they will think hard and, maybe, start a conversation like, "When did we meet last?" or "ages since we met", the idea being to find out about you.

D. *The last category consists of people who have not the foggiest idea about your identity:* Smile at them, and they will ask themselves the question "why is he smiling at me?" Perhaps they will blame their memory for forgetting and say to themselves "maybe he is someone important to me; it will be bad if he starts thinking I do not care". This can, and usually does, start a chain. The smile has made him spare time and brain power to think about you.

Have a positive attitude. When a communication is made to you, the first inclination should be to agree. This is because there is no such thing as an absolute truth, there are only perceptions. When rooms are allotted in a hostel, some may find the room comfortable, some too small and some may consider it next to paradise.

In a newspaper, as in any kind of team work, each group of tradesmen thinks it is the key. Reporters think they are the cock of the walk, subeditors think they are the ones who fashion the final product out of raw material supplied by reporters, and printers think they are really the ones who create. In fact, subeditors think reporters are only providers of the raw materials and printers are only technicians. They themselves are the creators. Ignoring any of them, or telling off one, can mean a bad paper, late production, mediocrity or sometimes no production at all. Give everybody importance by smiling at them, and half the battle is won.

If you have re-established/strengthened links by smiling at the other fellow, he will not have the feeling that you come only when you need him. Try to be helpful when the other fellow needs you. That is the safest insurance that he will cooperate when you need him.

Applications

It is part of the Theory of the Smile to present compliments, personal and professional. The compliments should relate to the plus points that you notice in a person. They must not be insincere.

There is a two-point hypothesis on which this is based.

First, every person has his/her plus and minus points. If one focuses on the minus points, that has been described by psychologists as Theory X. On the other hand one can focus on the plus points of a person and this has been described as Theory Y. Until some time ago employers, managers and others thought that theory X was the one which could get people to work harder, produce more and ensure or improve quality.

The latest thinking is that getting to stress the plus points of people makes them produce more and better.

If a reporter had earlier filed a great story, tell him how you would like a story of the same quality today. You will get results. If you harp on the bad news stories that he has filed, you will make no progress.

The second point of this hypothesis can be made in seven words:

Say "yes" rather than "no" whenever possible

This is important in life for everyone, but for journalists it is vital. Reporters create news sources by saying "yes" whenever possible. Subeditors, Chief Subeditors and News Editors create human relations which become unbreakable and enable them to perform feats of production unthinkable otherwise—just by saying "yes".

When you say "yes", it does not mean you are giving the other fellow a blank cheque. All that it means is that you are willing to go along to the extent possible.

Now look at the many executives and top management people who go about with a frown on the face rather than a smile. All that it means is that they are unwilling to go the extra mile to help solve a problem. For a time it creates fear in subordinates. In many cases the subordinates start imagining the boss is much too erudite to mix with them but the time comes, as it is bound to come in every case, when the individual subordinate thinks he knows all that is needed to know. He discovers that the big boss has nothing extra by way of erudition but his frown.

Management Skill

The fact is that the big boss has taken the easy way out by thinking, as his father did, that Theory X works by way of increased production and better quality. He is either too old or too lazy to learn that Theory Y, properly applied, works better.

Any journalist who becomes Editor/Deputy Editor/News Editor/ Chief of Bureau/Chief Reporter/Chief Subeditor reaches this position after long stints as a reporter/subeditor. Cynicism is the commonest ailment that afflicts journalists after a time. Most start thinking after a decade they know everything that is needed to be known to become a practitioner of Advanced journalism. The fact is that it is only after a decade or so that a journalist—not every journalist but those who want to rise to directing positions—comes to realise that Advanced Journalism is more about management and directing news gathering or production operations than about the technical skills mastered by subeditors and reporters.

The categorisation of management style into Theory X and Theory Y was made by McGregor (1960). Behind each of the theories are two different beliefs and assumptions about subordinates. Theory X style leaders believe that most people dislike work and will avoid it wherever possible. Such leaders feel they themselves are a small but important group who want to lead and take responsibility. Therefore, this style of leadership exercises strong controls and direction and wherever possible punishes people if they do not do the work.

Self-starters

Theory Y leaders assume that people will work hard and assume responsibility if they can satisfy their personal needs and the objectives or goals of their organisation. Such leaders do not sharply distinguish between the leaders and the followers in contrast to the Theory X style. They feel that people control themselves rather than waiting to be controlled by others—such as a leader or a manager or a supervisor.

An effective leader needs to examine carefully his own ideas about the motivation and behaviour of subordinates and others, as well as the situation, before adopting a particular style of leadership.

Applied to Advanced Journalism, Theory Y means you set the parameters and give the reporters/subeditors plenty of elbow room so that they can work in their own ideas into the task. It can, and frequently does, work wonders.

This is because the experienced head is not always, and not necessarily, the wisest. This has to be realised. It is not always realised.

There is a book named "How to get people to be self-starters." It is written by Thomas and Connellan. It sets out the most modern thinking on management which postulates in a nutshell that "if you let one know what great expectations are there from him, he will try to live up to them."

ABC Analysis

This is directly opposite to Theory X which believes the great majority of subordinates "want to be directed and avoid responsibility".

Pareto's law states that in any large number, there are a "significant few" and the "insignificant many". In fact, in any large number of people (or materials), there are three categories:

Category A: These are small in number but contribute 70% to 80% of the value. The practitioner of Advanced Journalism concentrates on them.

Category B: These are larger in number than *Category A* manpower or materials but make a sizeable contribution by way of quality and quantity. The practitioner of Advanced Journalism devotes a fair amount of attention to them, but much less than he devotes to *Category A* personnel/materials.

Category C: These personnel/materials make a minimal contribution to production/quality. The practitioner of Advanced Journalisiii devotes only marginal attention to them.

Pareto postulated, after an empirieal analysis, that something like 20% of the items in any sample account for 80% of the total cost as well as results annually in terms of materials and efforts. These are the significant few which require utmost attention.

This figure shows a typical ABC analysis in terms of percentage of number of inventory items and percentage of average inventory

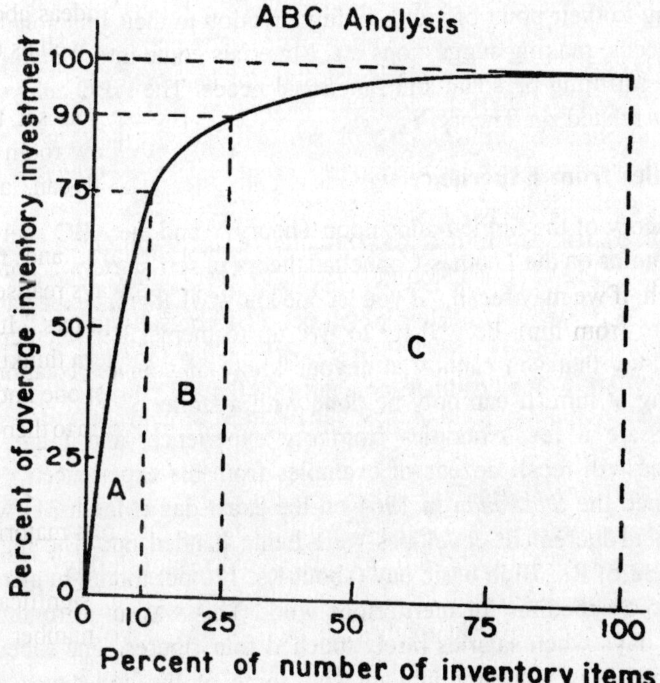

investment (annual usage value). Annual usage value is the demand multiplied by unit price, thus giving the monetary worth of annual consumption. It can be seen from this figure that 10% the items are claiming 65% of the annual usage value and thus constitute the "significant few." These are called A-class items.

Another 10% of items account for another 15% of annual usage value and are called B-class items. The vast majority of 75% of the items account for only 10% of the expenditure and effort and constitute the "insignificant many" and are called C-class items.

Once the items are grouped into A, B and C class we can adopt different degrees of seriousness in our efforts. A-class items require almost continuous and rigrous control. B-class items may have relaxed control and C-class items may be procured using simple rules of thumb.

Though the ABC analysis as originally propounded applies to materials, it is equally applicable to the personnel controlled by practitioners of Advanced Journalism. They concentrate on A-class personnel and functionaries and pay lavish attention to them. The "attention" primarily consists of smiling, encouraging, counselling, listening to their point of view, giving attention to their functional and other needs, making suggestions etc. Materials come into it mainly by way of fulfilling personal and functional needs. The ABC analysis is directly related on Theory Y.

Examples from Experience

The Theory of the Smile builds upon Theory Y and the ABC analysis. It also builds on the Thomas-Connellan theory of self-starters, according to which, if we may recall, "if you let one know what great expectations are there from him, he will try to live up to them". It is elementary psychology that you cannot let anyone know of your expectation by frowning at him. It can only be done with a smile.

Here are a few examples from my experience, and I am sure everyone will recall dozens of examples from his experience.

I joined the *Statesman* in 1964 on the exact day (March 31) when the annual increment envelopes were being handed out. The highest increment of Rs. 70 in basic pay (about Rs. 120 per month in all) was given to a subeditor for meritorious work. This was an astronomical sum in days when salaries rarely touched four figures. The subeditor concerned was naturally jubilant and some of his colleagues were jealous.

A week later the subeditor concerned was found to have done some shoddy work. The Resident Editor, Pran Chopra, sent him a note which read "Remember, you have a reputation to protect." The person concerned, always a good worker, became meticulous.

The same Pran Chopra a few months later put up on the notice board an extra-bright headline with the marginal remark "A strong contender in a contest we should have—headline of the week". No money was involved, but the glow on the face of the subeditor who had given the headline had to be seen to be believed.

In 1991 I was commissioned to edit *Communication-2000 AD,* the silver jubilee commemorative volume of the Indian Institute of Mass Communication. To assist me on the editorial side was recruited Nandini Prasad, a lady in her thirties who had done several jobs for short periods while she raised a family. She had no editorial experience to speak of and had forgotten the subediting symbols which she had learnt when a student at the IIMC 1977. But with her children now going to school she was very keen to make up for lost time by working extra hard.

I told her the rudiments of editing. For the rest, I kept encouraging her and smiling. She learnt mainly by observing me at work. We started work on the book in mid-February. The book had to be in hand—edited, printed and bound—by April 20 for the annual convocation. We thus had about seven weeks in all. In those seven weeks, Nandini matured from a virtual beginner in editing to someone on whom I leaned heavily for support by the sixth and seventh weeks.

I wonder what Nandini thinks of those seven hectic weeks, but I fondly hope those words of encouragement and praise which I used and which were always well deserved, and the constant smiling at each other, made a great contribution to her development as a professional.

When the book was produced, I found that Nandini and I started being considered editorial wizards. Seasoned faculty members who had worked for a dozen years or more started bringing their copy to us for "retouching". This was nothing new to me—I had been working for more then three decades. But for Nandini it must have been a new sensation. Today she is doing valuable work for a research institution and has written two books. She was on to her third book at the time of writing.

In yet another case, B. Venkateswara Rao, who started as the juniormost subeditors when the Delhi edition of *MID-DAY* was launched on March 31, 1986, became in 1992 the News Editor of a major edition of the *Indian Express*, later rising to be Resident Editor. All the learning was done by him; my contribution was to encourage and smile and praise and let him observe how things are done.

Key Catalysts

The moral is that while the blood and sweat, toil and tears are of the person concerned, Theory Y, the ABC analysis, the Theory of the Smile and the Thomas-Connellan theory of self-starters act as a catalyst. They are catalyses of course, but they are necessary for things to happen. With them also things may not happen in many cases. But in cases in which things do happen, the catalyst is needed. Or, at least, it makes things doubly fast. Frequently the absence of the catalyst prevents things from happening.

Finally, here is something which most people fail to observe but which is a necessary complement of the Theory of the Smile.

One day a foreign student, Ibrahim Rameez, a mid-carrier journalist from Maldives who came to attend the 19th Non-Aligned News Agency Journalism course at the Indian Institute of Mass Communication, observed as a I entered class: "You look handsome today."

I was the same man who had been entering the class for a month and a half to teach Advanced News Agency Journalism to the mid-career journalists from 14 foreign countries who had joined the course. Maybe the safari suit I was wearing was better pressed that day than my clothes on other days, maybe the colour and texture of the cloth suited may personality better. But my immediate reaction was, "Ibrahim, we have known each other for a month and a half. It is only today that you find me handsome".

'Handsomer', not 'Handsome'

It so happened that Ibrahim was seconded in his observation by Manal Abdul Aziz Ali of Egypt. Both were taken aback by my reply.

The pitfall of paying such a compliment, if you carefully evaluate it, is this: It may mean "you look handsome today, which was not the case for the past month and a half".

Therefore, the proper way to pay a personal compliment—if you are convinced you are paying the compliment appropriate to the occasion—is "you look handsomer today."

The difference is subtle but vital. If it occurred to me, it could occur to many more people. What is meant as a compliment may turn out to be a left-handed compliment.

I did not mind, of course, because I am a teacher. But there can be younger people with a fatter ego who may take it to heart.

The moral is: Every man is handsome in his own way, sometimes he may look more handsome; likewise, every woman is beautiful in her own way, sometimes she may look more beautiful.

EVER YOUNG

"Much of the credit for renovating the *Pioneer* goes to Mr. Desmond Young", writes Dr. S. N. Ghosh, the first Indian Editor of the paper (1946-72) in "*The Pioneer Saga",* the commemorative volume brought out on the 125th anniversary of the paper. "He planned the overnight move from Allahabad to Lucknow in 1933 when the paper came under Indian management... .

"The *Pioneer* made history for the entire newspaper world when it shifted from Allahabad to Lucknow, a distance of 140 miles, with machinery weighing 250 tons and a staff of 250 without missing a single issue, as planned and executed by Mr. Desmond Young in collaboration with the enthusiastic staff."

The first issue in Lucknow had the banner headline, "Good morning Lucknow, we are here".

CHAPTER XVII

Editing Skills for 2000 AD and After

The number of copies of newspapers sold in the United States in 1945 was 135 for every 100 households. That is, more than one per household. In 1989, according to the US Bureau of Census, the figure was 67 for every 100 households. It appears that many people have started thinking that the capsulised version of news and current affairs provided by TV/radio is good enough for them.

The trend has been evident for at least a decade and it has sparked off a flurry of innovations in newspaper editing.

To begin with, Editors of newspapers have come to realise that the high and mighty image of themselves was illusory. The new wisdom is that the newspaper is essentially a consumer product and one has to give the reader what he needs, or create a need and then fulfil it, in order to survive competition.

Audience Review

The first result of this realisation is a review of the audience. The conventional wisdom was that the Editor serviced the intellectuals, the advertisement department serviced trade and industry and thereby obtained advertising, and the circulation department serviced lay readers.

The daily was the Editor's paper, the advertisement department helped provide the wherewithal by humouring trade and industry and the circulation department sold it to whoever was interested in learning of the editorial wisdom.

This could, and frequently did, lead to mutually contradictory positions, specially in countries like India. To take a crude example, a

Reproduced from the futuristic volume, Communication-2000 AD, published by Indian Institute of Mass Communication, New Delhi, and edited by Adarsh Kumar Varma.

mass circulation paper in India, sold largely among those riding bicycles or managing with radios, had no place in it for advertisements for cars, vacuum cleaners and such other things. Yet advertisement managers tended increasingly to humour and service manufacturers of and traders in high-value items like cars, scooters, vacuum cleaners, even computers, in the hope of making big money.

Needless to say, advertisers became wiser after a time, and the paradox of different departments of a newspaper trying to service different audiences showed.

Some time in the 70s, it dawned on people that the different departments of a newspaper should coordinate their activities and try to service the same audience. If the Editor produces a paper largely for those travelling by bus and buying low-cost consumer durables, the advertisement manager has to approach manufacturers of and traders dealing in the same goods, and the circulation manager has to reach the paper to those whose interests it caters for.

Readers' Paper

It took time to sink in. And so, slowly, from the Editor's paper that most of the Indian dailies had been up to the sixties, they tended increasingly to become readers' papers. In the late 70s and early 80s, our dailies passed through a transitional phase when they tended to become reporters' papers. This was because of the unusual political happenings—Mrs. Gandhi's disqualification from Parliament, the JP movement, the Emergency, the Janata phase and the return of Mrs. Gandhi—which yielded tremendous opportunities to enterprising reporters and to those reporters who were willing to take sides.

Those who watched the media scene in the fifties, the sixties and earlier would recall how the major newspapers were linked to the names of famous editors—K. Rama Rao, C.Y. Chintamani, M. Chalapathi Rau, Devadas Gandhi, Frank Moraes, S.N. Ghosh, S. Sadanand, etc.

When the *National Herald* of Lucknow held its silver jubilee celebrations in 1963, Jawaharlal Nehru visited Lucknow specially for the occasion. In his speech, he told the distinguished audience: "Some say the *Herald* is Nehru's paper, others that it is the Congress paper, still others that it is the people's paper. The reality is that it is Chalapathi Rau's paper. Whatever he makes of it, that is the *Herald*".

Nehru was not being polite. A decade earlier, when Feroze Gandhi was the *Herald's* Managing Director, there were differences of opinion between him and Chalapathi Rau. Chalapathi Rau sent in his resignation. It was not accepted. Instead Feroze Gandhi, Nehru's son-in-law, was removed from the *Herald* and found a job with the *Express* in Delhi.

Prem Saxena, who later rose to be a high-profile Business Manager of the *Pioneer* in Kanpur, giving it business worth a million rupees a month, told me in 1985 of another tell-tale incident which took place in 1958. Saxena was in 1958 a junior Advertisement Department functionary in the *National Herald* with the job of placing the various advertisements booked into various pages. On Diwali eve, he found many advertisers clamouring for their advertisements to be carried on Page 1. He obliged five of them, filling up almost half of the Diwali front page of the *Herald* with advertising.

When the advertisement dummy reached Chalapathi Rau in the normal course at 5:30 p.m. he promptly crossed out four of the advertisements and retained only one which conformed to the size of the daily Page 1 advertisement. He then signed the dummy and sent it back to Saxena.

Saxena thought that with the big man so annoyed he had no future in the *Herald.* He went home and told his wife he must get another job.

Fright of Editors

Such was the fright of Editors in days when daily newspapers were as much known by the Editor's name as by their own name. The fact that this is make-believe has been progressively brought home to the world—and to Editors themselves—in the past two decades. Readers have increasingly taken to asserting their preferences regardless, and sometimes in defiance, of what the Editor chooses to give them.

Apart from content, reader preference has been progressively reflected in form. The double-decker headline with a double-column intro for display items, which gave every page a vertical look, has yielded to a sweeping horizontal look. Stories are now displayed in three, four or more columns one below the other, leaving plenty of white space around the headlines to make them stand out.

S. Mulgaokar, as Editor of the *Hindustan Times,* pioneered this revolution with the help of experts from the International Press

Institute. His initiative was immediately followed up by the *Indian Express,* and a little later by *Patriot,* the *National Herald* and still later by the *Statesman* and the *Times of India.*

This revolution is now petering out. Two new concepts are sweeping in. One is the Entry Point concept and the other the Total Page Concept (TPC).

Newspapers are getting more and more voluminous and readers are increasingly being rushed for time. With TV and radio giving the news neatly packaged, many readers find it increasingly irksome to try to locate where the major local (or international or national or sports) news is. The reason is that in the case of TV and radio, the audience has basically a passive role. In the case of newspapers, readers have to locate the items of their interest. This has given birth to the Entry Point concept.

Entry Points can be (a) to the paper or (b) to a story.

Entry Points to Paper

A house meant for a family has normally two Entry Points—one at the front and the other at the back (sometimes at the side). That suffices for the five, six or at the most dozen members of the family.

What do you do if the family consists of 50,000 or 100,000 members? If there are only two Entry Points to a house for such a huge family, most members would have to spend hours walking several kilometres to any of the two Entry Points in order to reach their living quarters.

They should be pardoned if some of them resent this effort and wish to migrate to other living quarters where entry is easier.

This is the rationale of the Entry Points concept. For, the modern day newspaper is increasingly becoming a joint dwelling unit for thousands of readers who have different preferences.

In India, the national newspapers have graduated to editions of 20 to 24 pages whereas earlier the average was 12 to 16. Still earlier it was 8 to 10. On Saturdays and Sundays, and often on weekdays too, there are special pullouts and other reading material numbering eight or more pages.

In more affluent countries, editions of several score pages are not uncommon.

To make it easier for the average reader to locate the items of his interest in this sea of information, newspapers are progressively devoting space, attention and energy to creating additional Entry Points, mostly on Page 1.

These Entry Points consist not merely of an index but of graphics, attractive headlines, blurbs which give the story away or pretend that they hide more than they bare, pointers, pictures, matrices, tell-tale quotes from stories going inside, cartoons, sketches, colour—anything to lure the reader to "enter" the inside pages instead of reading the latest news on the front page and putting the paper away in order to hear the TV news.

Why Entry Points

There are papers in the world which give so much importance to these Entry Points that they devote as much as one-third of Page 1 to them, managing all the advertising and the spot news meant for Page 1 within the remaining space.

Apart from telling the reader exactly where to find things of his interest, these Entry Points give a big psychological advantage to the newspaper concerned. Most readers read only one or two stories on Page 1, glancing at the headlines of the rest or taking in snatches of others. When they see, through pictorial representation, cartoons, sketches, blurbs, quotes, etc., attractive media messages, it registers on the brain.

The average reader who has read one story in full and snatches of four other stories will still find himself thinking the paper is very newsy if some 8 or 10 brief messages from the Entry Points register on the brain. Without the Entry Points the impact on his brain is of 3 or 4 news items.

Selection of the Entry Points is a skilled job. Representation of them without using up too much of space through message/sketch/blurb/quote/picture is even more specialised. Since the daily newspaper is like a house for thousands or lakhs of readers, the Entry Points should give a variety of messages, making sure that only the best in the particular section are represented, and they are represented in a way to lure the reader best. It is for the reader to enter a particular page or section looking for the story whose glimpse in the Entry Points enchanted him.

No reader can possibly read 20 or 24 pages of printed matter, what to say of more voluminous editions which are not infrequent. To look for the matter of one's choice is an additional irritant. By giving Entry Points to the paper, the Editor is at once lightening the burden of the reader in locating items of his interest and, simultaneously, indicating to him which pages and stories he may enter, depending upon his interest, given the limited time he wants to spend reading the daily newspaper.

To revert to the example of Entry Points to a house, each person or group of persons will prefer the Entry Points which are nearest his living quarters.

Inside Box

Everyone must have noticed the Entry Points which prestigious magazines like *India Today* and *Sunday* provide to the reader, complete with colour pictures, tell-tale quotes and tantalising blurbs. Daily newspapers are trying to follow suit and have learnt not to feel hampered by lack of staff and time. The earlier mindset allowed the front page to be packed only with news. Now everyone will find the Delhi editions of most English dailies trying to give Entry Points to connected stories on, for instance, the Gulf crisis, inserted in the main story on the subject on Page 1.

The movement towards giving Entry Points on Page 1 of daily papers is at least two decades old. Many papers at one time gave a small "Inside" box on Page 1. In the 1970s, when I was a Chief Sub at the *Statesman*, New Delhi, I started a campaign to give skilfully written pointers on page 1 to important stories on inside pages. At one point I was giving 8 to 10 pointers on page 1 each day. But I found that, since other Chief Subs did not do so the subeditors of my team thought it was a fad of mine. The result was that I was reduced to giving all the pointers myself—which is a kingsize job in itself since the penalty for going wrong is prohibitive.

Interestingly, the News Editor and the Editor, while appreciating my effort, never got into the spirit of it. The other Chief Subs were not given instructions to provide similar Entry Points to the reader. Secondly, when I proposed logistical arrangements to provide to me pictures and sketches at the relevant time (about midnight in the case of the main edition), they only laughed.

The *Statesman* thus missed a chance to be a pioneer in this field. It was *India Today* which took the lead, and now the daily newspapers are ahead of it in providing Entry Points. The daily which lays out the extra money and effort to provide sufficient and attractive Entry Points will, I have no doubt, score over its rivals.

A few years later, when I was the Editor of the *Pioneer,* I was able to implement my Entry Points project with great success. In fact this was one of the reasons why, when I wanted to return to New Delhi, the *Pioneer* dangled many blandishments to make me stay on. But that is another story.

Entry Points to Story

Just as the whole Communication Package (the daily newspaper) needs several Entry Points to it, the major individual news items, particularly the running stories, may also have several Entry Points.

Visualise a hypothetical situation where Prime Minister Chandra Shekher (or any other Prime Minister) holds a meeting of leaders of various parties to discuss a weighty national problem. The headline will only say they discussed the problem, differed or arrived at a consensus. But the observant reporter notes that he reserved a bear hug for a former Prime Minister but turned his face away when another former Prime Minister offered his hand.

Now this piece of significant observation can be put in a sidebar (or side story); it can be shown in a photograph if the photographer was alert; or the relevant sentence can be lifted from the report and converted into a blurb to be inserted into the story. All the three can serve as a second Entry Point to the story, the first being the headline.

Many a reader will yawn if the story says *Party leaders differ on Kashmir* or some such thing; they always differ on most issues. But most will be lured into reading the main story if there is a blurb or a sidebar indicating the different treatments given by the Prime Minister to two important political leaders.

Even if the latest story, which is expected to be on Page 1 with other connected stories on inside pages, yields no such sidebar, blurb or picture, a juicy but less important connected story going on an inside page can yield a valuable Entry Point which can lure the reader to enter not only the inside page story but the Page 1 story itself.

Suppose the Prime Minister holds a press conference and answers questions on subjects as different from each other as chalk from cheese. The most important answer (or answers), making policy announcements, will go on Page 1. It is possible that the Prime Minister flares up at a question on an unimportant topic. This, along with other less important parts of the press conference, may go on an inside page. But a sketch of an angry Prime Minister with a suitable blurb of a few tell-tale words can lure the reader not only to the inside page stuff but to the Page 1 story itself.

The *Illustrated Weekly of India,* in its December 22-23 issue of 1990, carried a report on the Ram Janmabhoomi-Babri Masjid controversy. There are as many as 9 Entry Points to the report including pictures and boxes and the headline. Not only this, Entry Point 9, going on the last page, has an Entry Point to itself—an Entry point within an Entry Point.

Entry Point Within Entry Point

To make a confession, I was myself not impressed by the headline *City Under Siege* given to the box item and was skipping it. Then I saw the picture of the Maulvi who led the last prayer at Babri Masjid in 1949 and changed my mind. I read *City Under Siege* directly as a result of the Entry Point within an Entry Point.

As the 21st century advances, Entry Points both to the newspaper and to the important individual stories will become more common. And as the bulk of the daily paper increases and the time the reader can spare progressively diminishes, I expect such Entry Points to become the rule. Dailies and periodicals which resist the change will suffer—as the *Statesman* suffered in the 60s when it stuck obstinately for several years to the double-decker headline with a double-column intro. Ultimately it had to go along with the sweeping horizontal make-up.

Another major advance in editing is the Total Page Concept (TPC). Steven E. Ames, in his early 1989 book *Elements of Newspaper Design,* defines TPC as editors so organising a page "that the reader can easily identify the importance of news".

Oldtime journalists will acidly remark, "Oh, but this is what we always tried to do". Agreed. Ames has elaborated on how to do it, but so fast is the concept catching on that the 1989 thoughts of Ames now look rather uncrystallised.

Modules

The fact is that, traditionally, Editors, News Editors and Chief Subs have tended to identify stories by their importance and news value, giving them priority—lead, second lead, and so forth. They have also tried to put connected stories together—like a story connected to lead to be given as *leg to lead* or *top to go with lead.*

TPC, as developed further since 1989, postulates that the newsfall of any given day can be classified into five or six modules. In the Gulf War situation, there could be, say, the following modules:

1. The *Gulf crisis* (political, military and other stories from many world centres).
2. *Local reports* (say 30,000 new phone lines for city, major and minor crime, power and water supply, a sensational murder, a major court judgement, etc.)
3. *Sports* (including, say, an Indo-Pak Test, Supersoccer, tennis in which Leander Paes and other Indians are taking part, major international hockey matches, etc.)
4. *National politics (ministry*-making, govt. decisions, politicking, etc.)
5. *Reports from states*
6. *Terrorism, secessionism*
7. *Neighbours* (Sri Lanka, Bangladesh, etc.)
8. *Lifestyle.*

What TPC means is that the Editor-in-Charge (maybe News Editor, maybe the Chief Sub, or partly the first and partly the second) makes up his mind which module yields the biggest, most voluminous and most juicy news. He allocates, say, 33 per cent of Page 1 to that, with 20 per cent to the next most important and maybe 15 per cent each to three other modules.

Now the 33 per cent of space allocated to the most newsy module (according to the day's newsfall) gives not only the most important story or stories of the module but also blurbs and other Entry points to the story *plus* Entry Points to the stories of the module going on inside pages.

This way, the editor is refraining from exercising his judgement as between individual stories; he is only indicating to the reader which area of the day's newsfall looks the most interesting to him. After this, the reader is free to choose which module to enter first, which next, which last and which not at all.

Three important points have to be noted in this connection:

1. The relative importance of various modules can, and frequently does, change on different days depending on the newsfall. Accordingly the position on Page 1 also changes.

2. Some modules may yield nothing worth Page 1 (for instance the *Reports from states* module). If that is so, Entry Points to *Reports from states* on inside pages can go into the the *Terrorism, secessionism* module which pertains to Punjab, Kashmir, Assam, etc.

3. Economic affairs can be a separate module, but frequently they are the result of something in other modules (*Gulf crisis, National politics*). In the latter case, any economic news worth Page 1 goes into the particular module of which it is the fallout (also Entry Points to economic stories on inside pages).

Big Advantage

A major advantage of the modular approach is that once having decided on the relative importance of various modules, the Editor-in-Charge (or his successor) can go on modifying the package in particular modules for replating or for subsequent editions without disturbing the whole page.

The modern computer-based technology makes it possible to make quick changes for successive editions with virtually no loss of time. Block-making is eliminated.

In the fourth and fifth generation computers, even the cutting and pasting of bromide paper, which was necessary when first and second generation photosetting were introduced, has been done away with. Make-up is done by computer and whole pages (or parts of pages which can be put together) can be outputted.

The total effect of these two concepts—Entry Points (for the whole paper as well as for individual modules/stories) and Total Page Concept or TPC—is that newspaper production is becoming increasingly dependent on Advanced Journalism.

Further Reading

1. UGC's Academic Staff College 1991 papers, BHU, Varanasi.
2. Management of Organisational Behaviour by Paul Hersey and Kenneth H. Blanchard.
3. Arms, Aims and Objects by Gen. J.N. Chaudhuri.
4. Out of My Mind by Sudhir Dar.
5. Sheer Anecdotage: Leaves from a Reporter's Diary by D.R. Mankekar.
6. UNI—1961-71 Commemorative Volume.
7. UNI—1971-81 Commemorative Volume.
8. UNI—1961-86 Silver Jubilee Commemorative Volume.
9. The Judgement by Kuldip Nayar.
10. A Long Innings by Vijay S. Hazare.
11. The Pioneer Saga 1865-1989, 125th Year Commemorative Volume.
12. Communication 2000 AD, Silver Jubilee Commemorative Volume of the Indian Institute of Mass Communication, edited by Adarsh Kumar Varma.
13. Your Slip is Showing by S. Nihal Singh.
14. How to Grow People into Self-Starters by Thomas and Connellan.
15. S.T.E.P.S. for Success by Gordon Wainright.
16. Leadership Rules: Doing the Right Thing rather than Doing Things Right by Michael Shea.
17. Cases in Consumer Behaviour by Hale N. Tongren.
18. The 22 Immutable Laws of Marketing by Al Ries and Jack Trout.
19. Making the Most of Yourself by Gill Cox and Sheila Dainow.

Index